Study Guide
to accompany
ACCOUNTING PRINCIPLES

Fifteenth Edition

Fess • Warren

Prepared by
James A. Heintz, DBA, CPA
Professor of Accounting
Indiana University, Bloomington

Carl S. Warren, PhD, CPA, CMA
Professor of Accounting
University of Georgia, Athens

Published by

A307 **SOUTH-WESTERN PUBLISHING CO.**

CINCINNATI   WEST CHICAGO, IL   DALLAS   LIVERMORE, CA

CONTENTS

Chapter		Page Problems	Page Solutions
1	Accounting Principles and Practices	1	169
2	The Accounting Cycle	11	172
3	Completion of the Accounting Cycle	25	175
4	Accounting for a Merchandising Enterprise	39	179
5	Periodic Reporting for a Merchandising Enterprise	53	182
6	Deferrals and Accruals	67	186
7	Accounting Systems Design	75	190
8	Cash	87	194
9	Receivables and Temporary Investments	97	196
10	Inventories	109	198
11	Plant Assets and Intangible Assets	121	201
12	Payroll, Notes Payable, and Other Current Liabilities	133	204
13	Concepts and Principles	145	207
14	Partnership Formation, Income Division, and Liquidation	155	209

Chapter 1

ACCOUNTING PRINCIPLES AND PRACTICES

STUDY GOALS

After studying this chapter, you should be able to:
1. Define accounting as an information system.
2. List the users of accounting information.
3. Describe the accounting profession and its specialized fields.
4. Explain what is meant by the business entity concept and the cost principle.
5. Define each of the three elements of the accounting equation and list the various forms of the equation.
6. Using an accounting equation format, record basic types of business transactions in terms of changes in the elements of the equation.
7. Prepare the basic financial statements for a sole proprietorship and corporation.

GLOSSARY OF KEY TERMS

Accounting. The process of identifying, measuring, and communicating economic information to permit informed judgments and decisions by users of the information.

Accounting equation. The expression of the relationship between assets, liabilities, and owner's equity; most commonly stated as Assets = Liabilities + Owner's Equity.

Account form of balance sheet. A balance sheet with assets on the left-hand side and liabilities and owner's equity on the right-hand side.

Account payable. A liability created by a purchase made on credit.

Account receivable. A claim against a customer for sales made on credit.

American Institute of Certified Public Accountants (AICPA). The national professional organization of CPAs.

Asset. Property owned by a business enterprise.

Balance sheet. A financial statement listing the assets, liabilities, and owner's equity of a business entity as of a specific date.

Bookkeeping. The recording of business data in a prescribed manner.

Business entity concept. The concept that assumes that accounting applies to individual economic units and that each unit is separate and distinct from the persons who supply its assets.

Business transaction. The occurrence of an event or of a condition that must be recorded in the accounting records.

Certified Public Accountant (CPA). An accountant who meets state licensing requirements for engaging in the practice of public accounting as a CPA.

Codes of professional ethics. Standards of conduct established by professional organizations of CPAs to guide CPAs in the conduct of their practices.

Corporation. A separate legal entity that is organized in accordance with state or federal statutes and in which ownership is divided into shares of stock.

Cost principle. The principle that assumes that the monetary record for properties and services purchased by a business should be maintained in terms of cost.

Dividend. A distribution of earnings of a corporation to its owners (stockholders).

Equity. The right or claim to the properties of a business enterprise.

Expense. The amount of assets consumed or services used in the process of earning revenue.

Financial Accounting Standards Board (FASB). The current authoritative body for the development of accounting principles for all entities except state and municipal governments.

Generally accepted accounting principles (GAAP). Generally accepted guidelines for the preparation of financial statements.

Income statement. A summary of the revenues and expenses of a business entity for a specific period of time.

Liability. A debt of a business enterprise.

Net income. The final figure in the income statement when revenues exceed expenses.

Net loss. The final figure in the income statement when expenses exceed revenues.

Owner's equity. The rights of the owners in a business enterprise.

Partnership. An unincorporated business owned by two or more individuals.

Prepaid expense. A purchased commodity or service that has not been consumed at the end of an accounting period.

Private accounting. The profession whose members are accountants employed by a business firm or nonprofit organization.

Public accounting. The profession whose members render accounting services on a fee basis.

Report form of balance sheet. The form of balance sheet with the liability and owner's equity sections presented below the asset section.

Retained earnings. Net income retained in a corporation.

Retained earnings statement. A statement for a corporate enterprise, summarizing the changes in retained earnings during a specific period of time.

Revenues. The gross increase in owner's equity as a result of business and professional activities entered into for the purpose of earning income.

Sole proprietorship. A business owned by one individual.

Statement of changes in financial position. A basic financial statement devoted exclusively to reporting changes in financial position for a specified period of time.

Stockholders' equity. The equity of the shareholders in a corporation.

CHAPTER OUTLINE

I. Accounting as an Information System.
  A. Accounting is an information system that provides essential information about the financial activities of an entity to various individuals or groups for their use in making informed judgments and decisions.
  B. Accounting information is composed principally of financial data about business transactions, expressed in terms of money.
II. Users of Accounting Information.
  A. Accounting provides the techniques for gathering economic data and the language for communicating these data to different individuals and institutions.
  B. Those individuals charged with the responsibility for directing the operations of enterprises, management, depend upon and make the most use of accounting information.
  C. The process of using accounting to provide information to users involves (1) identification of user groups and their information needs, (2) the gathering and processing of economic data by the accounting system, and (3) the generation of reports communicating the information to users.
III. Relationship of Accounting to Other Fields.
  A. Individuals engaged in all areas of business need not be expert accountants, but they are more effective if they have an understanding of accounting principles.
  B. The importance of understanding accounting is not limited to the business world, but extends to nonbusiness areas such as engineering, law, etc.
IV. Opportunities in Accounting.
  A. Accounting has experienced rapid development during this century.
  B. Factors contributing to the increased growth of accounting include the increase in number, size, and complexity of business organizations; frequent changes in the tax laws; and other governmental restrictions on business operations.
V. Profession of Accountancy.
  A. Accountancy is a profession whose members may be viewed as engaged in either (1) private accounting or (2) public accounting.
    1. Accountants employed by a particular business firm or not-for-profit organization are said to be engaged in private accounting. The certificate in management accounting (CMA) and the certificate in internal auditing (CIA) recognize the professional competency of private accountants.
    2. Accountants who render accounting services on a fee basis are said to be engaged in public accounting.
      a. Public accountants who meet state laws may become certified public accountants (CPAs).
      b. CPAs must adhere to professional codes of ethics.
  B. The specialized fields of accounting include

the following: financial accounting, auditing, cost accounting, managerial accounting, tax accounting, accounting systems, budgetary accounting, international accounting, not-for-profit accounting, social accounting, and accounting instruction.

VI. Bookkeeping and Accounting.
   A. Bookkeeping is the recording of business data in a prescribed manner.
   B. As distinguished from bookkeeping, accounting is primarily concerned with the design of the system of records, preparation of reports based on the recorded data, and the interpretation of the reports.

VII. Principles and Practice.
   A. The development of accounting principles is a never-ending process.
   B. Based upon research, accepted accounting practices, and professional pronouncements, generally accepted accounting principles evolve to form an underlying basis for accounting practice.

VIII. Business Entity Concept.
   A. The business entity concept is based on the applicability of accounting to individual economic units in society.
   B. Businesses are customarily organized as sole proprietorships, partnerships, or corporations.

IX. The Cost Principle.
   A. Under the cost principle, monetary accounting records are expressed in terms of cost.
   B. The exchange price, or cost, agreed upon by buyer and seller, determines the monetary amount to be recorded.

X. Business Transactions.
   A. A business transaction is the occurrence of an event or of a condition that must be recorded.
   B. Transactions that do not directly relate to outsiders are sometimes referred to as internal transactions.

XI. Assets, Liabilities, and Owner's Equity.
   A. The properties owned by a business enterprise are referred to as assets and the rights or claims to the properties are referred to as equities.
   B. Equities may be subdivided into two principal types: the rights of creditors (called liabilities) and the rights of owners (called owner's equity).
   C. The accounting equation may be expressed in the following ways: assets = equities; assets = liabilities + owner's equity; assets − liabilities = owner's equity.

XII. Transactions and the Accounting Equation.
   A. All business transactions can be expressed in terms of the resulting change in the three basic elements (assets, liabilities, and owner's equity) of the accounting equation.
   B. A purchase on account is a type of transaction that creates a liability, account pay-

able, in which the purchaser agrees to pay in the near future.
   C. Consumable goods purchased are considered to be prepaid expenses or assets.
   D. The amount charged to customers for goods or services sold to them is called revenue.
   E. A sale on account allows the customer to pay later and the selling firm acquires an account receivable.
   F. The amount of assets consumed or services used in the process of earning revenues is called expense.
   G. In recording the effect of transactions on the accounting equation, the following observations should be noted:
      1. The effect of every transaction can be stated in terms of increases and/or decreases in one or more of the accounting equation elements.
      2. The equality of the two sides of the accounting equation is always maintained.
      3. The owner's equity is increased by amounts invested by the owner and is decreased by withdrawals by the owner.
      4. Owner's equity is increased by revenues and is decreased by expenses.

XIII. Accounting Statements.
   A. The income statement is the summary of the revenue and expenses of a business entity for a specific period of time.
      1. The excess of revenue over expenses incurred in earning the revenue is called net income or net profit.
      2. If the expenses of the enterprise exceed the revenue, the excess is a net loss.
      3. In the determination of periodic net income, the expenses incurred in generating revenues must be properly matched against the revenues generated.
   B. The statement of owner's equity summarizes the changes in owner's equity that have occurred during a specific period of time.
      1. Three types of transactions may affect owner's equity during the period: (1) investments by the owner, (2) net income or net loss for the period, and (3) withdrawals by the owner.
      2. The statement of owner's equity serves as a connecting link between the balance sheet and the income statement.
   C. The balance sheet lists the assets, liabilities, and owner's equity of a business as of a specific date.
      1. The form of balance sheet with the liability and owner's equity section presented below the asset section is called the report form.
      2. The form of balance sheet which lists assets on the left and liabilities and owner's equity on the right is called the account form of balance sheet.

3. Assets are listed in the order in which they will be converted into cash or used up in the near future.
4. In the balance sheet, liabilities are reported first, followed by owner's equity.
D. The statement of changes in financial position is also useful in appraising a business enterprise and is discussed and explained in a later chapter.
E. The statements for corporations which have many owners (called stockholders) differ slightly from those of sole proprietorships.
1. Instead of a statement of owner's equity, changes in retained earnings (resulting from net income and distribution of earnings, called dividends) are reported in a retained earnings statement for a corporation.
2. The balance sheet for a corporation includes a stockholders' equity section which lists capital stock and retained earnings.

PART 1

Instructions: A list of terms and related statements appear below. From the list of terms, select the one that relates to each statement and print its identifying letter in the space provided.

A. Account payable
B. Account receivable
C. Accounting equation
D. Assets
E. Balance sheet

F. Cost principle
G. Equities
H. Expense
I. Income statement
J. Liabilities

K. Net income
L. Owner's equity
M. Prepaid expenses
N. Revenue
O. Statement of owner's equity

_F_ 1. The records of properties and services purchased by a business are maintained in accordance with the (?)

_D_ 2. The properties owned by a business enterprise.

_G_ 3. The rights or claims to the properties owned by a business enterprise.

_J_ 4. The rights of creditors represent debts of the business and are called (?)

_L_ 5. The rights of the owner or owners.

_C_ 6. Assets = Liabilities + Owner's Equity

_A_ 7. The liability created by a purchase on account.

_M_ 8. Consumable goods purchased, such as supplies, are considered to be assets or (?)

_N_ 9. The amount charged to customers for goods or services sold to them.

_B_ 10. When sales are made on account, allowing the customer to pay later, the business acquires an (?)

_H_ 11. The amount of assets consumed or services used in the process of earning revenue.

_E_ 12. A list of the assets, liabilities, and owner's equity of a business entity as of a specific date, usually at the close of the last day of a month or year.

_I_ 13. A summary of the revenue and expenses of a business entity for a specific period of time, such as a month or year.

_O_ 14. A summary of the changes in the owner's equity of a business entity that have occurred during a specific period of time, such as a month or year.

_K_ 15. The excess of revenue over the expenses incurred in earning the revenue is called (?)

PART 2

Instructions: Indicate whether each of the following statements is true or false by placing a check mark in the appropriate column.

	True	False
1. Accounting is often characterized as the "language of business."	X	
2. Accountants who render accounting services on a fee basis, and staff accountants employed by them, are said to be engaged in private accounting.		X
3. Standards of conduct which have been established to guide CPAs in the conduct of their practices are called codes of professional responsibility.		X
4. Accounting systems is the special field concerned with the design and implementation of procedures for the accumulation and reporting of financial data.	X	
5. Bookkeeping is primarily concerned with the design of the system of records, the preparation of reports based on the recorded data, and the interpretation of the reports.		X
6. A separate legal entity, organized in accordance with state or federal statutes and in which ownership is divided into shares of stock, is referred to as a corporation.	X	
7. A partnership is owned by not less than four individuals.		X
8. A business transaction is the occurrence of an event or of a condition that must be recorded.	X	
9. A summary of the changes in the owner's equity of a business entity that have occurred during a specific period of time, such as a month or a year, is called a statement of changes in financial position.		X
10. Distributions of earnings to owners (stockholders) are called dividends.	X	

PART 3

Instructions: Complete each of the following statements by circling the letter of the best answer.

1. Accountants employed by a particular business firm or nonprofit organization, perhaps as chief accountant, controller, or financial vice-president, are said to be engaged in
   a. general accounting
   b. public accounting
   c. independent accounting
   (d.) private accounting

2. Authoritative accounting pronouncements on accounting principles are issued by the
   a. Accounting Principles Commission
   b. Accounting Procedures Committee
   (c.) Financial Accounting Standards Board
   d. General Accounting Principles Board

3. The records of properties and services purchased by a business are maintained in accordance with the
   a. corporate principle
   (b.) cost principle
   c. matching principle
   d. proprietorship principle

4. Another way of writing the accounting equation is
   a. Assets + Liabilities = Owner's Equity
   b. Owner's Equity + Assets = Liabilities
   c. Assets = Owner's Equity − Liabilities
   (d.) Assets − Liabilities = Owner's Equity

5. The form of balance sheet with the liability and owner's equity sections presented below the asset section is called the
   (a.) report form
   b. balancing form
   c. account form
   d. systematic form

PART 4

Instructions: Some typical transactions of Cho Company are presented below. For each transaction, indicate the increase (+), the decrease (−), or no change (o) in the assets (A), liabilities (L), and owner's equity (OE) by placing the appropriate sign(s) in the appropriate column(s). More than one sign may have to be placed in the A, L, or OE column for a given transaction.

	A	L	OE
1. Issued capital stock for cash	+	o	+
2. Purchased supplies on account	+	+	−
3. Charged customers for services sold on account	+	o	+
4. Received cash from cash customers	+	o	+
5. Paid cash for rent on building	−	o	−
6. Collected an account receivable in full	+−		+
7. Paid cash for supplies	−+	−	−
8. Returned supplies purchased on account and not yet paid for	−	−+	−
9. Paid cash to creditors on account	+	−	−
10. Paid cash dividends to stockholders	−	−	−

7

PART 5

Instructions: The assets, liabilities, and owner's equity of Ted Brown, who operates a small repair shop, are expressed in equation form below. Following the equation are 10 transactions completed by Brown. On each of the numbered lines, show by addition or subtraction the effect of each of the transactions on the equation. For each transaction, identify the changes in owner's equity by placing the letter R (revenue), E (expense), D (drawing), or I (investment) at the right of each increase or decrease in owner's equity. On the lines labeled "Bal.", show the new equation resulting from the transaction.

	Assets			=	Liabilities	+	Owner's Equity
	Cash	+ Supplies	+ Land	=	Accounts Payable	+	Ted Brown, Capital

1. Brown started a repair shop and deposited $24,000 cash in the bank for use by the business.

(1) ~~24000~~ R   I   24,000 I

2. Brown purchased $2,400 of supplies on account.

(2)   2400   E   2400

Bal. 24000 + 2400

3. Brown purchased land for a future building site for $12,000 cash.

(3) −12000   +12000

Bal. 12000 + 2400 + 12000   2400   24000

4. Brown paid creditors $800 on account.

(4) − 800   − 800 E

Bal. 11,200 + 2400 + 12000   1600   24000

5. Brown withdrew $1,500 for personal use.

(5) −1500 D   − 1500 D

Bal. 9700 + 2400 + 12000   22,500

6. Brown paid $2,000 for building and equipment rent for the month.

(6) −2000 E   − 2000 E

Bal. 7700   2400   12000   1600   20,500

7. During the month, another $600 of expenses were incurred on account by the business.

(7)   + 600   − 600 E

Bal. 7700   2400   12000   2200   19,900

8. During the month, Brown deposited another $24,000 of personal funds in the business bank account.

(8) 24000 I   24000 I

Bal. 31700   2400   12000   2200   43900

9. Brown received $140 for a cash service call.

(9) + 140 R   140 R

Bal. 31840   2400   12000   2200   44040

10. Brown used $200 worth of supplies.

(10)   − 200   − 200 E

Bal. 31840   2200   12000   2200   43840

8

PART 6

John Miller started John's Lawnmower Service on January 1, 1987, at which time he invested $7,500 in the business. During the year, he withdrew $8,250 for personal use.

The assets and liabilities as of December 31, 1987, and the revenues and expenses for the year are as follows:

Cash	$ 6,000
Accounts receivable	3,750
Supplies	700
Accounts payable	1,300
Sales	22,450
Rent expense	4,600
Advertising expense	3,375
Utilities expense	3,000
Supplies expense	450
Miscellaneous expense	1,125

Instructions: Using the forms provided, prepare the following:
(1) An income statement for the year ended December 31, 1987.
(2) A statement of owner's equity for the year ended December 31, 1987.
(3) A balance sheet as of December 31, 1987.

(1)

John's Lawnmower Service
Income Statement
For Year Ended December 31, 1987

Sales Earned				22450 00	
Operating Expenses					
Rent	4600 00				
adv. Exp.	3375 00				
Utilities	3000 00				
Supplies	450 00				
misc	1125 00	12550 00			
Net Income				9900 00	

(2)

John's Lawnmower Service
Statement of Owner's Equity
For Year Ended December 31, 1987

John's L. Service, capital		7500 —	
Net Income for yr. ending Dec. 31, 1987	9900 —		
withdrawals	8250 —		
Increase in owners equity		1650	
		9150	

(3)

John's Lawnmower Service
Balance Sheet
December 31, 1987

	Assets			
	Cash		6000	
	Accts Receivable		3750	
	Supplies		700	
	Total assets		10450	
	Liabilities			
	Accts. Payable		1300	
	Owners Equity			
	Johns L.S. capital		9150	
	Total liabilities + O.E.		10450	

Chapter 2

THE ACCOUNTING CYCLE

STUDY GOALS

After studying this chapter, you should be able to:
1. Explain what an account is and how transactions can be recorded in accounts.
2. Explain what is meant by the double-entry accounting method of recording transactions.
3. List the general rules of debit and credit and normal balances for asset, liability, owner's equity, revenue, expense, drawing, and dividend accounts.
4. List the common classifications of accounts for a small service enterprise.
5. Prepare a chart of accounts for a small service enter-prise.
6. Diagram the flow of accounting data through an accounting system.
7. Record business transactions using a two-column journal, a two-column account, and a four-column account.
8. Post transactions from a two-column journal to the ledger.
9. Prepare a trial balance and explain its use in the discovery of errors.

GLOSSARY OF KEY TERMS

Account. The form used to record additions and deductions for each individual asset, liability, owner's equity, revenue, and expense.

Account payable. A liability created by a purchase made on credit.

Account receivable. A claim against a customer for sales made on credit.

Balance of an account. The amount of difference between the debits and the credits that have been entered into an account.

Capital. The rights (equity) of the owners in a business enterprise.

Capital stock. Shares of ownership of a corporation.

Cash. Any medium of exchange that a bank will accept at face value.

Chart of accounts. A listing of all the accounts used by a business enterprise.

Credit. (1) The right side of an account; (2) the amount entered on the right side of an account; (3) to enter an amount on the right side of an account.

Current asset. Cash or another asset that may reasonably be expected to be realized in cash or sold or consumed, usually within a year or less, through the normal operations of a business.

Current liability. A liability that will be due within a short time (usually one year or less) and that is to be paid out of current assets.

Debit. (1) The left side of an account; (2) the amount entered on the left side of an account; (3) to enter an amount on the left side of an account.

Double-entry accounting. A system for recording transactions based on recording increases and decreases in accounts so that debits always equal credits.

Drawing account. The account used to record distributions to a sole proprietor or partner.

Journal. The initial record in which the effects of a transaction on accounts are recorded.

Journalizing. The process of recording a transaction in a journal.

Ledger. The group of accounts used by an enterprise.

Long-term liability. A liability that is not due for a comparatively long time (usually more than one year).

Net worth. The owner's equity in a business.

Nominal account. A revenue or expense account periodically closed to the income summary account; a temporary owner's equity account.

Note payable. A written promise to pay, representing an amount owed by a business.

Note receivable. A written promise to pay, representing an amount to be received by a business.

Plant asset. A tangible asset of a relatively fixed or permanent nature owned by a business enterprise.

Posting. The process of transferring debits and credits from a journal to the accounts.

Prepaid expense. A purchased commodity or service that has not been consumed at the end of an accounting period.

Real account. A balance sheet account.

Slide. The erroneous movement of all digits in a number, one or more spaces to the right or the left, such as writing $542 as $5,420.

Stockholders' equity. The equity of the shareholders in a corporation.

T account. A form of account resembling the letter T.

Temporary account. A revenue or expense account periodically closed to the income summary account; a nominal account.

Transposition. The erroneous arrangement of digits in a number, such as writing $542 as $524.

Trial balance. A summary listing of the balances and the titles of the accounts.

CHAPTER OUTLINE

I. Nature of an Account.
   A. For purposes of recording individual transactions, a record called an account is used. A group of related accounts is called a ledger.
   B. Accounts have the following characteristics:
      1. A title, which is the name of the item recorded in the account.
      2. A space for recording increases in the amount of the item, in terms of money.
      3. A space for recording decreases in the amount of the item, in terms of money.
      4. The simplest form of the account is known as the T account.
      5. The left side of an account is called the debit side.
      6. The right side of an account is called the credit side.
      7. Amounts entered on the left side of the account are called debits or charges to the account.
      8. Amounts entered on the right side of the account are called credits to the account.
      9. The notation indicating the sum of the debits and the sum of the credits entered directly below the debit and credit column is referred to as a pencil footing.
      10. Subtraction of the smaller of the total debits or credits from the larger amount will yield the balance of an account.
      11. The balance of an account will either be a debit balance or a credit balance.
   C. Recording transactions in balance sheet accounts (asset, liability, and owner's equity accounts) includes the following considerations:
      1. Every business transaction affects a minimum of two accounts.
      2. Transaction data are initially entered in a record called a journal.
      3. The process of recording a transaction in the journal is called journalizing and the form of presentation is called a journal entry.
      4. The data in the journal entry are transferred to the appropriate accounts by a process known as posting.
      5. An entry composed of two or more debits or two or more credits is called a compound journal entry.
      6. The equality of debits and credits for each transaction is inherent in the accounting equation and is known as double-entry accounting.
      7. The rules of debit and credit for balance sheet accounts may be stated as follows: *Debit* may signify:
      Increase in asset accounts
      Decrease in liability accounts
      Decrease in owner's equity accounts
      Credit may signify:
      Decrease in asset accounts
      Increase in liability accounts
      Increase in owner's equity accounts
      8. The rules of debit and credit for balance sheet accounts may also be stated in relationship to the accounting equation as follows:

Asset Accounts	
Debit for increases	Credit for decreases

=

Liability Accounts	
Debit for decreases	Credit for increases

+

Owner's Equity Accounts	
Debit for decreases	Credit for increases

      9. Withdrawals from an owner are recorded as debits to a drawing account.
      10. Dividends of a corporation are recorded as debits to a dividends account.
   D. Transactions in income statement accounts (revenue and expense accounts) are recorded in the following manner:

1. Increases in revenue accounts are recorded as credits. Decreases are recorded as debits.
2. Increases in expense accounts are recorded as debits. Decreases are recorded as credits.
3. The rules for debit and credit for income statement accounts are summarized below:

Debit for
decreases in owner's equity

Expense Accounts

Debit for increases	Credit for decreases

Credit for
increases in owner's equity

Revenue Accounts

Debit for decreases	Credit for increases

4. At the end of an accounting period, the revenue and expense account balances are reported in the income statement.
5. At the end of the accounting period, the revenue and expense account balances are transferred to a summarizing account and the accounts are said to be closed.
6. Accounts which are closed at the end of an accounting period are called temporary or nominal accounts.
7. The balances of balance sheet accounts are carried forward from year to year and are referred to as real accounts.

II. Normal Balances of Accounts.
   A. The sum of the increases in an account is usually equal to or greater than the decreases in an account and therefore an account is said to have a normal balance.
   B. The rules of debit and credit and the normal balances of balance sheet and income statement accounts are summarized as follows:

	Increase	Decrease	Normal Balance
Balance sheet accounts:			
Asset	Debit	Credit	Debit
Liability	Credit	Debit	Credit
Owner's Equity:			
Capital, Capital Stock, Retained Earnings	Credit	Debit	Credit
Drawing, Dividends	Debit	Credit	Debit
Income statement accounts:			
Revenue	Credit	Debit	Credit
Expense	Debit	Credit	Debit

III. Classification of Accounts.
   A. Accounts in the ledger are customarily listed in the order in which they appear in the financial statements and are classified according to common characteristics.
   B. An asset is any physical thing (tangible) or right (intangible) that has a money value.
      1. Current assets are assets that may reasonably be expected to be realized in cash or sold or used up within a year or less through the normal operations of the business. Current assets normally include cash, notes receivable, accounts receivable, and prepaid expenses.
      2. Tangible assets that are of a permanent or fixed nature are called plant assets or fixed assets. Plant assets normally include equipment, machinery, buildings, and land.
   C. Liabilities are debts owed to outsiders (creditors) and are frequently described by the word payable.
      1. Current liabilities are liabilities that will be due within a short time (usually one year or less) that are to be paid out of current assets. Current liabilities normally include notes payable, accounts payable, salaries payable, interest payable, and taxes payable.
      2. Long-term liabilities are liabilities that will not be due for a comparatively long time (usually more than one year). As long-term liabilities become due within one year and are to be paid, they become current liabilities.
   D. Owner's equity is the residual claim against the assets of the business after the total liabilities are deducted. Owner's equity may be referred to as stockholders' equity, shareholders' equity, and stockholders' investment.
      1. Capital is the owner's equity in a sole proprietorship.
      2. For a corporation, capital stock and retained earnings represent owner's equity.
      3. Drawings represent the amount of withdrawals by the owner of a sole proprietorship and dividends represent the distribution of earnings to stockholders of a corporation.
   E. Revenues are the gross increases in owner's equity as a result of the sale of merchandise, the performance of services, the rental of property, or other income-earning activities.
   F. Expenses are costs that have been consumed in the process of producing revenue.

IV. Chart of Accounts.
   A. The number of accounts maintained by a specific enterprise is affected by the nature of its operations, its type of business, and the

extent to which details are needed for taxing authorities, managerial decisions, credit purposes, etc.

B. A listing of the accounts in the ledger is called a chart of accounts.

V. Flow of Accounting Data.

A. The flow of accounting data may be diagrammed as follows:

		Entry	Entry
		recorded in	posted to
Business	Business		
TRANSACTION→	DOCUMENT→	JOURNAL→	LEDGER
occurs	prepared		

B. The initial record of each transaction is a business document.

C. Transactions are entered in chronological order in the journal.

D. The amounts of the debits and credits in the journal are posted to the accounts in the ledger.

VI. Two-Column Journal.

A. Before a transaction is entered in the two-column journal, it should be analyzed according to the following steps:

1. Determine whether an asset, a liability, owner's equity, revenue, or expense is affected.

2. Determine whether the affected asset, liability, owner's equity, revenue, or expense increases or decreases.

3. Determine whether the effect of the transaction should be recorded as a debit or as a credit in an asset, liability, owner's equity, revenue, or expense account.

B. The process of recording a transaction in a two-column journal is summarized as follows:

1. Record the date:

a. Insert the year at the top only of the Date column of each page, except when the year date changes.

b. Insert the month on the first line only of the Date column of each page, except when the month date changes.

c. Insert the day in the Date column on the first line used for each transaction, regardless of the number of transactions during the day.

2. Record the debit:
Insert the title of the account to be debited at the extreme left of the Description column and enter the amount in the Debit column.

3. Record the credit:
Insert the title of the account to be credited below the account debited, moderately indented, and enter the amount in the Credit column.

4. Write an explanation:
Brief explanations may be written below

each entry, moderately indented. Some accountants prefer that the explanation be omitted if the nature of the transaction is obvious. It is also permissible to omit a lengthy explanation of a complex transaction if a reference to the related business document can be substituted.

VII. Two-Column Accounts and Four-Column Accounts.

A. Accounts in the simple T form are used primarily for illustrative purposes.

B. The addition of special rulings to the T form yields the standard two-column form and four-column form.

VIII. Posting.

A. The debits and credits in the journal may be posted in the order that they occur, or all the debits may be posted first, followed by the credits.

B. The posting of a debit journal entry or a credit journal entry to an account in the ledger is performed in the following manner:

1. Record the date and the amount of the entry in the account.

2. Insert the number of the journal page in the Posting Reference column of the account.

3. Insert the ledger account number in the Posting Reference column of the journal.

IX. Illustration of Journalizing and Posting.

A. The journalizing and posting process for a month's transactions is illustrated on pages 67-74 of the text.

B. To reduce repetition, some of the transactions are stated in summary form.

X. Trial Balance.

A. The equality of debits and credits in the ledger should be verified at the end of each accounting period through the preparation of a trial balance.

B. The trial balance does not provide complete proof of the accuracy of the ledger. It indicates only that the debits and credits are equal.

C. If the two totals of a trial balance are not equal, it is probably due to one or more of the following types of errors:

1. Error in preparing the trial balance, such as:

a. One of the columns of the trial balance was incorrectly added.

b. The amount of an account balance was incorrectly recorded on the trial balance.

c. A debit balance was recorded on the trial balance as a credit, or vice versa, or a balance was omitted entirely.

2. Error in determining the account balances, such as:

a. A balance was incorrectly computed.

b. A balance was entered in the wrong balance column.

3. Error in recording a transaction in the ledger, such as:

   a. An erroneous amount was posted to the account.

   b. A debit entry was posted as a credit, or vice versa.

   c. A debit or a credit posting was omitted.

D. Among the types of errors that will not cause inequality in the trial balance totals are the following:

   1. Failure to record a transaction or to post a transaction.

   2. Recording the same erroneous amount for both the debit and the credit parts of a transaction.

   3. Recording the same transaction more than once.

   4. Posting a part of a transaction correctly as a debit or credit but to the wrong account.

E. Two common types of errors are known as transpositions (an erroneous arrangement of digits) and slides (the movement of an entire number erroneously one or more spaces to the right or left).

F. The discovery of an error usually involves the retracing of the various steps in the accounting process.

PART 1

Instructions: A list of terms and related statements appear below. From the list of terms, select the one that relates to each statement and print its identifying letter in the space provided.

A. Current assets
B. Current liabilities
C. Journalizing
D. Ledger
E. Long-term liabilities

F. Nominal accounts
G. Owner's equity
H. Plant assets
I. Posting

J. Real accounts
K. Retained earnings
L. Stockholders' equity
M. Trial balance

___D___ 1. A group of related accounts that comprise a complete unit, such as all of the accounts of a specific business enterprise.

___C___ 2. The process of recording a transaction in the journal.

___I___ 3. The process by which the data in the journal entry are transferred to the appropriate accounts.

___F___ 4. Revenue and expense accounts which are transferred to a summarizing account at the end of the accounting year.

___J___ 5. The balances of the accounts reported in the balance sheet are carried forward from year to year and because of their permanence are sometimes referred to as (?)

___A___ 6. Assets that may reasonably be expected to be realized in cash or sold or used up usually within a year or less, through the normal operations of the business.

___H___ 7. Tangible assets used in the business that are of a permanent or relatively fixed nature are called (?)

___B___ 8. Liabilities that will be due within a short time (usually one year or less) and that are to be paid out of current assets.

___E___ 9. Liabilities that will not be due for a comparatively long time (usually more than one year) are called (?)

___G___ 10. The residual claim against the assets of the business after the total liabilities are deducted.

___L___ 11. For a corporation, owner's equity is frequently called (?)

___K___ 12. The net income retained in a corporation is termed (?)

___M___ 13. The equality of debits and credits in the ledger should be verified at the end of an accounting period, if not more often, by a(n) (?)

Name _____

PART 2

Instructions: Indicate whether each of the following statements is true or false by placing a check mark in the appropriate column.

	True	False
1. Amounts entered on the left side of an account, regardless of the account title, are called credits or charges to the account		X
2. The difference between the total debits and the total credits posted to an account yields a figure called the balance of the account	X	X
3. The two most frequently used classifications for presenting assets on the balance sheet are current assets and plant assets..	X	
4. Accounts receivable are claims against debtors evidenced by a written promise to pay a certain sum in money at a definite time to the order of a specified person or to bearer		X
5. The residual claim against the assets of a business after the total liabilities are deducted is called owner's equity	X	
6. Net income is the gross increase in owner's equity attributable to business activities	X	X
7. The process of recording a transaction in a journal is called posting		X
8. Revenue accounts are sometimes called temporary accounts	X	
9. A listing of the accounts in a ledger is called a chart of accounts	X	
10. A recording error caused by the erroneous rearrangement of digits, such as writing $627 as $672, is called a slide..		X

PART 3

Instructions: Complete each of the following statements by circling the letter of the best answer.

1. A journal entry composed of two or more debits or two or more credits is called a(n)
   a. multiple journal entry
   b. compound journal entry
   c. complex journal entry
   d. double journal entry

2. Periodically all revenue and expense account balances are transferred to a summarizing account and the accounts are then said to be
   a. closed
   b. balanced
   c. verified
   d. real

3. The drawing account of a sole proprietorship is comparable to which account of a corporation?
   a. retained earnings
   b. income summary
   c. owner's borrowing
   d. dividends

4. The equality of debits and credits in the ledger should be verified at the end of each accounting period by preparing a(n)
   a. accounting statement
   b. balance report
   c. trial balance
   d. account verification report

5. Of the following errors, the one that will cause an inequality in the trial balance totals is
   a. incorrectly computing an account balance
   b. failure to record a transaction
   c. recording the same transaction more than once
   d. posting a transaction to the wrong account

6. Drawing accounts are periodically closed to
   a. asset accounts
   b. capital accounts
   c. liability accounts
   d. expense accounts

7. Debits to expense accounts signify
   a. increases in owner's equity
   b. decreases in owner's equity
   c. increases in assets
   d. increases in liabilities

8. When rent is prepaid for several months in advance, the debit is to
   a. an expense account
   b. a capital account
   c. a liability account
   d. an asset account

9. When an asset is purchased on account, the credit is to
   a. a capital account
   b. a revenue account
   c. a liability account
   d. an expense account

10. When a payment is made to a supplier for goods previously purchased on account, the debit is to
   a. an asset account
   b. a liability account
   c. a capital account
   d. an expense account

18

PART 4

Eight transactions are recorded in the following T accounts:

Cash				Machinery		David Kim, Drawing	
(1)	9,000	(4)	2,000	(3) 4,500		(7) 3,000	
(8)	1,200	(7)	3,000				

Accounts Receivable				Accounts Payable		Service Revenue	
(5)	3,700	(8)	1,200	(4) 2,000	(2) 550		(5) 3,700
					(3) 4,500		
					(6) 980		

Supplies		David Kim, Capital		Operating Expenses	
(2) 550			(1) 9,000	(6) 980	

Instructions: For each debit and each credit, indicate in the following form the type of account affected (asset, liability, capital, drawing, revenue, or expense) and whether the account was increased (+) or decreased (−).

Transaction		Account Debited		Account Credited	
		Type	Effect	Type	Effect
(1)	9,000	asset	+	Capital	+
(2)	550	asset	+	Liab.	+
(3)	4,500	asset	+	Liab	+
(4)	2000	Liab	−	asset	−
(5)	3700	Acct Rec	+	Revenue	+
(6)	980	Opr Expense	+	Acct. Pay.	+
(7)	3000	Draw	+	asset	−
(8)	1200	asset	+	acct Rec	−

PART 5

During April of the current year, Ann Lewis started Ann's Service Co.

Instructions: (1) Record the following transactions in the general journal given below.

Apr. 3. Invested $23,000 in cash, equipment valued at $15,200, and a van worth $26,000.
Apr. 16. Purchased additional equipment on account, $6,000.
Apr. 29. Paid $2,800 to creditors on account.
(2) Post to the appropriate ledger accounts on the next page.
(3) Prepare a trial balance of the ledger accounts of Ann's Service Co. as of April 30 of the current year, using the form below.

(1)

JOURNAL

PAGE 1

DATE	DESCRIPTION	POST. REF.	DEBIT	CREDIT

(3)

Ann's Service Co.
Trial Balance
April 30, 19—

Name _____

LEDGER ACCOUNTS

ACCOUNT Cash   ACCOUNT NO. 11

DATE		ITEM	POST. REF.	DEBIT	CREDIT	BALANCE	
						DEBIT	CREDIT

ACCOUNT Equipment   ACCOUNT NO. 18

DATE		ITEM	POST. REF.	DEBIT	CREDIT	BALANCE	
						DEBIT	CREDIT

ACCOUNT Van   ACCOUNT NO. 19

DATE		ITEM	POST. REF.	DEBIT	CREDIT	BALANCE	
						DEBIT	CREDIT

ACCOUNT Accounts Payable   ACCOUNT NO. 22

DATE		ITEM	POST. REF.	DEBIT	CREDIT	BALANCE	
						DEBIT	CREDIT

ACCOUNT Ann Lewis, Capital   ACCOUNT NO. 31

DATE		ITEM	POST. REF.	DEBIT	CREDIT	BALANCE	
						DEBIT	CREDIT

PART 6

On January 2, 19—, Tom Teel, an attorney, opened a law office. The following transactions were completed during the month.

1. Invested $50,000 cash and $11,600 worth of office equipment in the business.
2. Paid a month's rent of $2,400.
3. Paid $1,300 for office supplies.
4. Paid secretary a salary of $2,200.
5. Collected legal fees of $19,600.
6. Bought an auto for business use. It cost $24,000. Sharp paid $6,000 down and charged the balance.
7. Paid $1,500 on accounts payable.
8. Withdrew $3,600 from the firm for personal use.
9. Paid $800 for auto repairs and maintenance.
10. Received a $240 electric bill.
11. Paid the $240 electric bill.
12. Paid premiums of $1,000 on property insurance.
13. Purchased $3,200 worth of additional office equipment on account.
14. Paid $800 cash for janitor service.
15. Paid $6,000 cash for books for the law library.

Instructions: (1) Record the transactions in the T accounts below. (2) Prepare a trial balance, using the form on the following page.

(1)

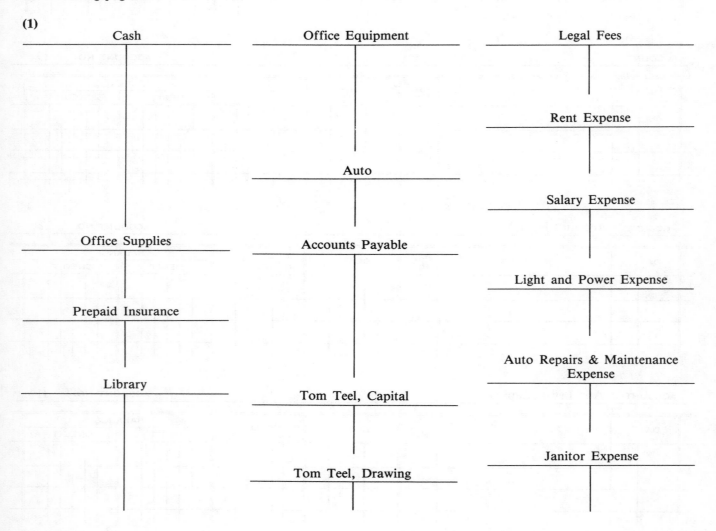

22

Name _____

(2)

Tom Teel
Trial Balance
January 31, 19—

Page not used

Chapter 3

COMPLETION OF THE ACCOUNTING CYCLE

STUDY GOALS

After studying this chapter, you should be able to:

1. Explain what is meant by the matching principle as it relates to the cash basis and the accrual basis of accounting.
2. Explain the nature of the adjusting process.
3. List the basic procedures for adjusting the accounting records prior to the preparation of the financial statements.
4. Prepare a work sheet for summarizing the accounting data for use in preparing financial statements of a service enterprise.
5. Prepare the basic financial statements of a service enterprise.
6. List the closing procedures for preparing the accounting records for use in accumulating data for the following accounting period.
7. Explain what is meant by a fiscal year and a natural business year.
8. Diagram the basic phases of the accounting cycle.

GLOSSARY OF KEY TERMS

Accounting cycle. The sequence of principal accounting procedures employed to process transactions during a fiscal period.

Accrual basis. Revenues are recognized in the period earned and expenses are recognized in the period incurred in the process of generating revenues.

Accrued expense. An expense accrued but unrecorded at the end of a fiscal period.

Accumulated depreciation account. The contra asset account used to accumulate the depreciation recognized to date on plant assets.

Adjusting entry. An entry required at the end of an accounting period to record an internal transaction and to bring the ledger up to date.

Cash basis. Revenue is recognized in the period cash is received, and expenses are recognized in period cash is paid.

Closing entry. An entry necessary to eliminate the balance of a temporary account in preparation for the following accounting period.

Contra account. An account that is offset against another account.

Depreciation. The decrease in usefulness of all plant assets except land.

Fiscal year. The annual accounting period adopted by an enterprise.

Income summary account. The account used in the closing process for summarizing the revenue and expense accounts.

Matching. The principle of accounting that all revenues should be matched with the expenses incurred in earning those revenues during a period of time.

Natural business year. A year that ends when a business's activities have reached the lowest point in its annual operating cycle.

Post-closing trial balance. A trial balance prepared after all of the temporary accounts have been closed.

Work sheet. A working paper used to assist in the preparation of financial statements.

CHAPTER OUTLINE

I. Matching Principle.
   A. At the end of an accounting period, the ledger accounts must be brought up to date to ensure that the revenues and expenses are properly matched, and the financial statements fairly present the results of operations for a period and the financial condition at the end of that period.
   B. Revenues and expenses may be reported on the income statement by the cash basis or the accrual basis of accounting.
   C. Most enterprises use the accrual basis of accounting.
   D. The accrual basis of accounting requires the use of the adjusting process at the end of the accounting period to properly match revenues and expenses for the period.

II. The Nature of the Adjusting Process.
   A. The entries required at the end of the accounting period to bring the accounts up to date and to ensure the proper matching of revenues and expenses are called adjusting entries.
   B. Items such as cost of supplies, prepaid rent, and other prepaid expenses of future periods are normally recorded initially as assets. At the end of the accounting period, that portion of the asset that has been consumed in the operations must be recorded by an adjusting entry debiting an expense account and crediting the asset account.
   C. The decrease in the usefulness of a plant asset is called depreciation. The adjusting entry to record depreciation is a debit to an expense account and a credit to a contra account, accumulated depreciation.
   D. An accumulated depreciation account is normally maintained for each plant asset except land, which does not depreciate.
   E. The difference between the balance of a plant asset account and the associated contra asset account (accumulated depreciation) is called the book value of the asset.
   F. Expenses which have accumulated but are unpaid and unrecorded at the end of an accounting period are referred to as accrued expenses.
   G. At the end of the accounting period, an adjusting entry debiting an expense account and crediting a liability account must be made for all accrued liabilities as of the last day of the accounting period.
   H. The failure to properly record adjusting journal entries at the end of the accounting period will misstate the financial statements for that period.

III. Work Sheet for Financial Statements.
   A. At the end of an accounting period, a work sheet may be prepared by the accountant to facilitate the preparation of the financial statements and the necessary adjusting journal entries.
   B. The trial balance columns of the work sheet are taken directly from the balances of the various ledger accounts at the end of the accounting period.
   C. The necessary debit and credit portions of the adjusting entries are entered on the work sheet in the adjustments columns.
   D. After the adjusting entries have been entered on the work sheet, the account balances are extended to the adjusted trial balance columns. The debit and credit columns are then totaled and compared to prove that no arithmetical errors have been made up to this point.
   E. The data in the adjusted trial balance columns are extended to the income statement and balance sheet columns of the work sheet. After all of the balances have been extended, each of the four columns is totaled. The net income or the net loss for the period is the amount of the difference between the totals of the two income statement columns. This net income or net loss is entered on the work sheet so that the income statement debit and credit columns and the balance sheet debit and credit columns balance.

IV. Financial Statements.
   A. The income statement columns of the work sheet are the source for all of the data reported on the income statement.
   B. The work sheet is the source for all the data reported on the statement of owner's equity, with the exception of any increases in the capital of a sole proprietorship which have occurred during the period. It is necessary to refer to the capital account in the ledger to determine the beginning balance and any such additional investments.
   C. The work sheet is the source of all the data reported on the balance sheet, with the exception of the amount of a sole proprietor's capital, which can be obtained from the statement of owner's equity. The stockholders' equity section of the balance sheet of a corporation requires the ending retained earnings, which can be obtained from the retained earnings statement.
   D. Normally all the data for preparation of the retained earnings statement of a corporation may be obtained from the balance sheet columns of the work sheet. If, however,

dividends are debited directly to the retained earnings account, the retained earnings account must be examined to determine the amount of dividends for the period.

V. Journalizing and Posting Adjusting Entries.
A. At the end of the accounting period, the adjusting entries appearing in the work sheet are recorded in the journal and posted to the ledger.
B. The process of journalizing and posting adjusting journal entries at the end of the accounting period brings the ledger into agreement with the data reported on the financial statements.

VI. Nature of the Closing Process.
A. The revenue, expense, and drawing (or dividends) accounts are temporary accounts used in classifying and summarizing changes in the owner's equity during the accounting period. At the end of the period, the net effect of the balances in these accounts must be recorded in the permanent capital account.
B. The transferring of the temporary account balances to the real accounts at the end of the accounting period is accomplished by a series of entries called closing entries.

VII. Journalizing and Posting Closing Entries.
A. An account titled Income Summary is used for summarizing the data in the revenue and expense accounts. It is used only at the end of the accounting period and is both opened and closed during the closing process.
B. The following four entries are required in order to close the temporary accounts of a sole proprietorship at the end of the period:
1. Each revenue account is debited for the amount of its balance, and Income Summary is credited for the total revenue.
2. Each expense account is credited for the amount of its balance, and Income Summary is debited for the total expense.
3. Income Summary is debited for the amount of its balance (net income), and the capital account is credited for the same amount. (Debit and credit are reversed if there is a net loss.)
4. The drawing account is credited for the amount of its balance, and the capital account is debited for the same amount.
C. After the closing entries have been journalized, the balance in the capital account will correspond to the amounts reported on the statement of owner's equity and the balance sheet. In addition, the revenue, expense, and

drawing accounts will have zero balances.
D. The procedure for closing the temporary accounts of a corporation differs only slightly from that of a sole proprietorship. Income Summary is closed to Retained Earnings, and Dividends is closed to Retained Earnings.

VIII. Post-Closing Trial Balance.
A. The last procedure of the accounting cycle is the preparation of a post-closing trial balance after all of the temporary accounts have been closed.
B. The purpose of the post-closing trial balance is to make sure the ledger is in balance at the beginning of the new accounting period. The accounts and amounts should agree exactly with the accounts and amounts listed on the balance sheet at the end of the period.

IX. Fiscal Year.
A. The maximum length of an accounting period is usually one year, which includes a complete cycle of the seasons of business activities.
B. The annual accounting period adopted by an enterprise is known as its fiscal year.
C. An accounting period ending when a business's activities have reached the lowest point in its annual operating cycle is termed the natural business year.
D. The long-term financial history of a business enterprise may be shown by a succession of balance sheets, prepared every year. The history of operations for the intervening periods is represented in a series of income statements.

X. Accounting Cycle.
A. The sequence of accounting procedures of fiscal period is called the accounting cycle.
B. The major phases of the accounting cycle as follows:
1. Transactions are analyzed and recorded a journal.
2. Transactions are posted to the ledger.
3. A trial balance is prepared, data nee adjust the accounts are assembled, a work sheet is completed.
4. Financial statements are prepared.
5. Adjusting and closing entries are ized.
6. Adjusting and closing entries are the ledger.
7. A post-closing trial balance is p
C. The most significant output of th ing cycle is the financial statemen

PART 1

Instructions: A list of terms and related statements appear below. From the list of terms, select the one that relates to each statement and print its identifying letter in the space provided.

A. Accrual basis
B. Accrued expense
C. Adjusting entries
D. Closing entries

E. Contra account
F. Depreciation
G. Fiscal year

H. Income summary
I. Natural business year
J. Post-closing trial balance

_____ 1. An accounting method in which revenues are reported in the period in which they are earned, and expenses are reported in the period in which they are incurred in an attempt to produce revenues.

_____ 2. The entries required at the end of an accounting period to bring the accounts up to date and to ensure the proper matching of revenues and expenses.

_____ 3. The allocation of the cost of an asset to expense over the accounting periods making up its useful life.

_____ 4. An account which is "offset against" another account.

_____ 5. An accumulated expense that is unpaid and unrecorded.

_____ 6. The balances are removed from the temporary accounts so that they will be ready for use in accumulating data for the following accounting period by means of (?)

_____ 7. An account that is used for summarizing the data in the revenue and expense accounts at the end of the accounting period.

_____ 8. A listing prepared in order to make sure that the ledger is in balance at the beginning of the new accounting period.

_____ 9. The annual accounting period adopted by an enterprise.

_____ 10. A period ending when a business's activities have reached the lowest point in its annual operating cycle.

Name _____

PART 2

Instructions: Indicate whether each of the following statements is true or false by placing a check mark in the appropriate column.

	True	**False**
1. Generally accepted accounting principles permit the use of either the cash or accrual basis of accounting.	___	___
2. When the reduction in prepaid expenses is not properly recorded, the asset accounts and expense accounts are overstated.	___	___
3. Accumulated depreciated accounts may be referred to as contra asset accounts.	___	___
4. When the Income Statement columns of the work sheet are totaled, and the Debit column total is greater than the Credit column total, the excess is the net income.	___	___
5. Dividend payments by a corporation can be debited either to Dividends or to Retained Earnings.	___	___
6. The adjusting entry to record depreciation of plant assets consists of a debit to a depreciation expense account and a credit to an accumulated depreciation account.	___	___
7. When services are not paid for until after they have been performed, the accrued expense is recorded in the accounts by an adjusting entry at the end of the accounting period.	___	___
8. A type of working paper frequently used by accountants prior to the preparation of financial statements is called a post-closing trial balance.	___	___
9. At the end of the period, the balances are removed from the temporary accounts and the net effect is recorded in the permanent account by means of closing entries.	___	___
10. The annual accounting period adopted by an enterprise is known as its current year.	___	___

PART 3

Instructions: Complete each of the following statements by circling the letter of the best answer.

1. Entries required at the end of an accounting period to bring the accounts up to date and to ensure the proper matching of revenues and expenses are called
   a. matching entries
   b. adjusting entries
   c. closing entries
   d. correcting entries

2. The decrease in usefulness of plant assets as time passes is called
   a. consumption
   b. deterioration
   c. depreciation
   d. contra asset

3. The difference between the plant asset account and the related accumulated depreciation account is called the
   a. book value of the asset
   b. approximate value of the asset
   c. net cost of the asset
   d. contra account balance of the asset

4. If a $250 adjustment for depreciation is not recorded, which of the following financial statement errors will occur?
   a. expenses will be overstated
   b. net income will be understated
   c. assets will be understated
   d. owner's equity will be overstated

5. The complete sequence of accounting procedures for a fiscal period is frequently called the
   a. work sheet process
   b. opening and closing cycle
   c. accounting cycle
   d. fiscal cycle

PART 4

Jim Morrison closes his books as of the end of each year (December 31). On April 1 of the current year, Jim insured the business assets for three years, at a premium of $5,000.

Instructions: (1) In the T accounts presented below, enter the adjusting entry that should be made by Morrison as of December 31 to record the amount of insurance expired as of that date. The April 1 premium payment is recorded in the T accounts.

Cash			Prepaid Insurance			Insurance Expense	
	Apr. 1	5,000	Apr. 1	5,000			

(2) Morrison's balance sheet as of December 31 should show the asset value of the unexpired
insurance as... $ _____

(3) Morrison's income statement for the year ended December 31 should show insurance expense
of .... $ _____

30

PART 5

  Kent Chase closes his books at the end of each month. Chase has only one employee, who is paid at the rate of $40 per day. The employee is paid every Friday at the end of the day. Each workweek is composed of five days, starting on Monday. Assume that the Fridays of this month (August) fall on the 7th, 14th, 21st, and 28th.

  Instructions: (1) Using the T accounts below, enter the four weekly wage payments for August. Then enter the adjusting entry that should be made by Chase as of August 31, to record the salary owed the employee but unpaid as of that date.

Cash	Salary Expense	Salaries Payable

(2) Chase's income statement for August should show total salary expense of . . . . $ _____

(3) Chase's balance sheet as of August 31 should show a liability for salaries payable of . . . . $ _____

Instructions: The journal, the income summary account, the sales account, and the expense accounts of Kathy Smith as of January 31 of the current year appear below. In the journal, prepare the entries to close Smith's revenue and expense accounts into the income summary account. Then post to the ledger.

JOURNAL

PAGE 8

DATE	DESCRIPTION	POST. REF.	DEBIT	CREDIT

ACCOUNT Income Summary   ACCOUNT NO. 36

DATE	ITEM	POST. REF.	DEBIT	CREDIT	BALANCE DEBIT	BALANCE CREDIT

ACCOUNT Sales   ACCOUNT NO. 47

DATE		ITEM	POST. REF.	DEBIT	CREDIT	BALANCE DEBIT	BALANCE CREDIT
19-- Jan	15		5		4 0 5 0 00		4 0 5 0 00
	31		6		1 1 4 3 0 00		1 5 4 8 0 00

ACCOUNT Salary Expense   ACCOUNT NO. 58

DATE		ITEM	POST. REF.	DEBIT	CREDIT	BALANCE DEBIT	BALANCE CREDIT
19-- Jan	31		6	7 2 0 0 00		7 2 0 0 00	

ACCOUNT Supplies Expense   ACCOUNT NO. 67

DATE		ITEM	POST. REF.	DEBIT	CREDIT	BALANCE DEBIT	BALANCE CREDIT
19-- Jan	15		5	2 3 4 0 00		2 3 4 0 00	
	25		6	1 7 1 0 00		4 0 5 0 00	
	31		6	1 0 8 0 00		5 1 3 0 00	

PART 7

The work sheet with the trial balance portion completed is given on pp. 34-35 for Rider Service Company for January.

Instructions: (1) Record the following adjustments in the Adjustments columns:
    (a) Salaries accrued but not paid at the end of the month amount to $980.
    (b) The $7,560 debit in the prepaid rent account is the payment of one year's rent on January 1.
    (c) The supplies on hand as of January 31 cost $1,400.
    (d) Depreciation of the tools and equipment for January is estimated at $560.
(2) Complete the work sheet.
(3) In the forms on pages 36-37, prepare an income statement, statement of owner's equity, and balance sheet.

	ACCOUNT TITLE	TRIAL BALANCE		ADJUSTMENTS	
		DEBIT	CREDIT	DEBIT	CREDIT
1	Cash	7 9 8 0 00			
2	Accounts Receivable	6 3 0 0 00			
3	Supplies	2 3 8 0 00			
4	Prepaid Rent	7 5 6 0 00			
5	Tools and Equipment	1 8 9 0 0 00			
6	Accumulated Depreciation		1 3 3 0 00		
7	Accounts Payable		6 1 6 0 00		
8	Gayle Rider, Capital		3 2 4 1 0 00		
9	Gayle Rider, Drawing	2 8 0 0 00			
10	Sales		2 4 8 5 0 00		
11	Salary Expense	1 3 7 9 0 00			
12	Miscellaneous Expense	5 0 4 0 00			
13		6 4 7 5 0 00	6 4 7 5 0 00		
14					
15					
16					
17					
18					
19					
20					
21					
22					
23					
24					
25					
26					
27					
28					
29					
30					
31					
32					
33					
34					
35					
36					
37					
38					
39					
40					
41					
42					

Name _____

Company _____

Sheet _____

January 31, 19 _____

ADJUSTED TRIAL BALANCE		INCOME STATEMENT		BALANCE SHEET		
DEBIT	CREDIT	DEBIT	CREDIT	DEBIT	CREDIT	
						1
						2
						3
						4
						5
						6
						7
						8
						9
						10
						11
						12
						13
						14
						15
						16
						17
						18
						19
						20
						21
						22
						23
						24
						25
						26
						27
						28
						29
						30
						31
						32
						33
						34
						35
						36
						37
						38
						39
						40
						41
						42

Rider Service Company
Income Statement
For Month Ended January 31, 19—

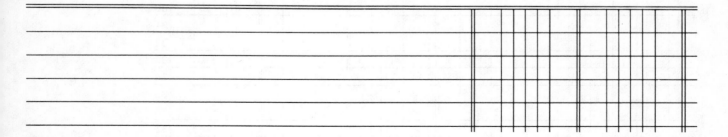

Rider Service Company
Statement of Owner's Equity
For Month Ended January 31, 19—

Name _____

Rider Service Company
Balance Sheet
January 31, 19—

Page Not Used

Chapter 4

ACCOUNTING FOR A MERCHANDISING ENTERPRISE

STUDY GOALS

After studying this chapter, you should be able to:
1. Explain and prepare general journal entries for purchases by a merchandising enterprise.
2. Explain and prepare journal entries for sales by a merchandising enterprise.
3. Explain the sequence of year-end procedures for a merchandising enterprise.
4. Explain the difference between the periodic and perpetual merchandise inventory systems.
5. Explain and prepare the merchandise sold section of an income statement.
6. Explain and prepare the journal entries for merchandise inventory adjustments at year end.
7. Prepare a completed work sheet for a merchandising enterprise.

GLOSSARY OF KEY TERMS

Cash discount. The deduction allowable if an invoice is paid by a specified date.

Credit memorandum. The form issued by a seller to inform a debtor that a credit has been posted to the debtor's account receivable.

Debit memorandum. The form issued by a buyer to inform a creditor that a debit has been posted to the creditor's account payable.

FOB destination. Terms of agreement between buyer and seller, whereby ownership passes when merchandise is received by the buyer, and the seller absorbs the transportation costs.

FOB shipping point. Terms of agreement betwen buyer and seller, whereby ownership passes when merchandise is delivered to the shipper, and the buyer absorbs the transportation costs.

Invoice. The bill provided by the seller (who refers to it as a sales invoice) to a buyer (who refers to it as a purchase invoice) for items purchased.

Periodic inventory system. A system of inventory accounting in which only the revenue from sales is recorded each time a sale is made; the cost of merchandise on hand at the end of a period is determined by a detailed listing (physical inventory) of the merchandise on hand.

Perpetual inventory system. A system of inventory accounting that employs records that continually disclose the amount of the inventory on hand.

Physical inventory. The detailed listing of merchandise on hand.

Purchases discounts. An available discount taken by the purchaser for early payment of an invoice; a contra account to Purchases.

Purchases returns and allowances. Reduction in purchases, resulting from merchandise returned to the vendor or from the vendor's reduction in the original purchase price; a contra account to Purchases.

Sales discounts. An available discount granted by the seller for early payment of an invoice.

Sales returns and allowances. Reductions in sales, resulting from merchandise returned by customers or from the seller's reduction in the original sales price.

Trade discount. The reduction allowable from the list price of goods offered for sale.

CHAPTER OUTLINE

I. Purchasing and Selling Procedures
  A. Merchandising enterprises acquire merchandise for resale to customers. It is the selling of merchandise, instead of a service, that makes the activities of merchandising enterprises differ from the activities of service enterprises.
  B. Although procedures in purchasing and selling merchandise vary from business to business, common procedures for recording transactions between buyers and sellers of merchandise exist.

II. Accounting for Purchases.
  A. Purchases of merchandise are accumulated in a purchases account by debiting Purchases.
  B. Discounts taken by the buyer for early payment of an invoice are called purchases discounts. They are recorded by crediting the purchases discounts account and are viewed as a deduction from the amount initially recorded as Purchases. In this sense, Purchases Discounts can be thought of as a contra (or offsetting) account to Purchases.
    1. The credit period during which the buyer is allowed to pay begins with the date of the sale as shown by the date of the invoice or bill.
    2. If the payment is due within a stated number of days after the date of invoice, for example, 30 days, the terms may be expressed as n/30. If payment is due at the end of the month, the terms may be expressed as n/eom.
    3. The terms 2/10, n/30 mean that, although the credit period is thirty days, the buyer may deduct 2% of the amount of the invoice if payment is made within ten days of the invoice date. This deduction is known as a cash discount.
    4. From the buyer's standpoint, it is important to take advantage of all available discounts, even though it may be necessary to borrow the money to make the payment.
  C. If merchandise is returned or a price adjustment is requested by the buyer, the transaction is recorded by a credit to a purchases returns and allowances account.
    1. The details of the merchandise returned or the price adjustment requested are set forth by the buyer in a debit memorandum.
    2. A confirmation from the seller of the amount of the merchandise returned or the price adjustment requested is set forth in a credit memorandum.
    3. The purchases returns and allowances account can be viewed as a deduction from the amount initially recorded as Purchases. In this sense, Purchases Returns and Allowances can be thought of as a contra (or offsetting) account to Purchases.
    4. When a buyer returns merchandise or has been granted an allowance prior to the payment of the invoice, the amount of the debit memorandum is deducted from the invoice amount before the purchases discount is computed.

III. Accounting For Sales.
  A. Merchandise sales are recorded by the seller by a credit to a sales account.
    1. Cash sales are recorded by a debit to Cash and a credit to Sales.
    2. Sales to customers who use bank credit cards are recorded as cash sales.
    3. Sales of merchandise on account are recorded by a debit to Accounts Receivable and a credit to Sales.
    4. Sales made by use of nonbank credit cards are recorded as sales on account. Any service fees charged by the card company are debited to Service Fee Expense.
  B. The seller refers to the discounts taken by the buyer for early payment of an invoice as sales discounts. These discounts are recorded by debiting the sales discounts account, which is viewed as a reduction in the amount initially recorded as Sales. In this sense, Sales Discounts can be thought of as a contra (or offsetting) account to Sales.
  C. Merchandise sold that is returned by the buyer or for which a price adjustment is made is recorded by the seller by debiting a sales returns and allowances account. This account is viewed as a reduction in the amount initially recorded as Sales. In this sense, Sales Returns and Allowances can be thought of as a contra (or offsetting) account to Sales.

IV. Trade Discounts.
  A. Manufacturers and wholesalers of certain types of merchandise give large reductions from list prices quoted in their catalogs. Such reductions are called trade discounts.
  B. There is no need to record list prices and their related trade discounts in the accounts. Only the agreed price (the list price net of the trade discount) is recorded in the accounts.

V. Transportation Costs.
  A. If the ownership of merchandise passes to the buyer when the seller delivers the merchandise to the shipper, the buyer is to absorb the transportation costs, and the terms are said to be FOB shipping point.
    1. Transportation costs paid by the buyer should be debited to Transportation In or Freight In and credited to Cash.

2. The balance of the transportation in or freight in account should be added to net purchases in determining the total cost of merchandise purchased.

3. Sellers may prepay the transportation costs and add them to the invoice, as an accommodation to the buyer. In this case, the buyer should debit Transportation In for the transportation costs and compute any purchases discounts on the amount of the sale rather than on the invoice total. The seller records the prepayment of transportation costs by adding the amount to the total invoice and debiting Accounts Receivable.

B. If ownership of the merchandise passes to the buyer when the merchandise is received by the buyer, the seller is to assume the costs of transportation, and the terms are said to be FOB destination.

  1. The amounts paid by the seller for delivery of merchandise are debited to Transportation Out, or Delivery Expense, or a similarly titled account.

  2. The total of such costs incurred during a period is reported on the seller's income statement as a selling expense.

VI. Sales Taxes.

A. Almost all states and many other taxing units levy a tax on sales of merchandise, which becomes a liability at the time the sale is made.

B. At the time of a cash sale, the seller collects the sales tax and credits a liability account, Sales Tax Payable. Periodically, the sales tax liability is paid to the taxing unit.

C. The buyer debits the Purchases account for the full amount of merchandise acquired, including the sales tax.

VII. Periodic Reporting for Merchandising Enterprises.

A. The sequence of year-end procedures for a merchandising enterprise are as follows:

  1. Prepare a trial balance of the ledger on a work sheet form.

  2. Review the accounts and gather the data required for the adjustments.

  3. Insert the adjustments and complete the work sheet.

  4. Prepare financial statements from the data in the work sheet.

  5. Journalize the adjusting entries and post to the ledger.

  6. Journalize the closing entries and post to the ledger.

  7. Prepare a post-closing trial balance of the ledger.

B. The summarizing and reporting procedures for a merchandising enterprise are similar to those of a service enterprise except for merchandise inventory.

VIII. Merchandise Inventory Systems.

A. Under the periodic inventory system, the revenues from sales are recorded when sales are made, but no attempt is made on the sales date to record the cost of merchandise sold.

  1. A detailed listing of merchandise on hand (called a physical inventory) is made at the end of the accounting period.

  2. The physical inventory at the end of the accounting period determines the cost of merchandise sold during the period and the cost of inventory on hand at the end of the period.

B. Under the perpetual inventory system, both the sales amount and the cost of merchandise sold amount are recorded when each item of merchandise is sold. In this manner, the accounting records continuously (perpetually) disclose the inventory on hand.

IX. Cost of Merchandise Sold.

A. Under the periodic inventory system, the cost of merchandise sold during a period is reported in a separate section of the income statement.

  1. Net purchases are determined by subtracting from the balance of the purchases account the balances of the purchases returns and allowances and purchases discounts accounts.

  2. The cost of merchandise purchased during the period is determined by adding to the net purchases the amount of transportation in incurred during the period.

  3. Merchandise available for sale is determined by adding the beginning merchandise inventory for the period to the cost of merchandise purchased during the period.

  4. The cost of merchandise sold for the period is determined by subtracting the ending merchandise inventory for the period from the merchandise available for sale.

B. The data necessary for the preparation of the cost of merchandise sold section of the income statement may be obtained from the balances of the ledger accounts for purchases, purchases returns and allowances, purchases discounts, transportation in, and merchandise inventory (beginning inventory). The amount for ending merchandise inventory is determined by a physical inventory.

X. Merchandise Inventory Adjustments.

A. At the end of the period, it is necessary to remove from Merchandise Inventory the amount representing the inventory at the beginning of the period and to replace it with the amount representing the inventory at the end of the period. This is accomplished by two adjusting entries.

  1. The first adjusting entry transfers the beginning inventory to Income Summary by

debiting Income Summary and crediting Merchandise Inventory for the beginning inventory.
2. The second adjusting entry debits the cost of merchandise inventory at the end of the period to Merchandise Inventory and credits the amount to Income Summary.
B. The effect of the two inventory adjustments is to transfer the beginning inventory amount to Income Summary as part of the cost of merchandise available for sale and to transfer the ending inventory amount to Income Summary as a deduction from the cost of merchandise available for sale.

XI. Trial Balance and Adjustments on the Work Sheet.
A. After year-end posting of the journal has been completed, a trial balance of the ledger is taken and transferred to a work sheet.
B. The adjustment data are placed on the work sheet in a manner similar to that of the service enterprise, with the exception of the two merchandise inventory adjustments.

XII. Completing the Work Sheet.
A. After all the necessary adjustments are entered on the work sheet, the two adjustments columns are totaled to prove the equality of the debits and credits.
B. The balances of the adjusted trial balance columns are then extended to the statement columns in a manner similar to that of a service enterprise, except that both the debit and credit amounts for Income Summary are extended to the income statement columns.
C. After all items have been extended to the statement sections of the work sheet, the four columns are totaled and the net income or net loss is determined in the normal manner.

XIII. Completion of Year-End Procedures.
A. The year-end accounting procedures that are necessary for a merchandising enterprise include the preparation of financial statements, adjusting entries, and closing entries.
B. The completion of the year-end procedures is described and illustrated in Chapter 5.

PART 1

Instructions: A list of terms and related statements appear below. From the list of terms, select the one that relates to each statement and print its identifying letter in the space provided.

A. Cash discount   **E.** FOB shipping point   **I.** Sales discounts
B. Credit memorandum   **F.** Periodic inventory system   **J.** Trade discounts
C. Debit memorandum   **G.** Perpetual inventory system
D. FOB destination   **H.** Purchases discounts

_____ 1. As a means of encouraging payment before the end of the credit period, a discount for the early payment of cash is known as a (?)

_____ 2. The general term for discounts taken by the buyer for early payment of an invoice is (?)

_____ 3. When merchandise is returned or a price adjustment is requested, the buyer may inform the seller through the use of a (?)

_____ 4. The document issued by the seller, allowing for returns of merchandise or a price reduction.

_____ 5. The seller refers to the discounts taken by the buyer for early payment of an invoice as (?)

_____ 6. Reductions from quoted list prices given by manufacturers and wholesalers of certain types of merchandise.

_____ 7. If the ownership of the merchandise passes to the buyer when the seller delivers the merchandise to the shipper, the buyer is to absorb the transportation costs, and the terms are said to be (?)

_____ 8. If ownership passes to the buyer when the merchandise is received by the buyer, the seller is to assume the costs of transportation, and the terms are said to be (?)

_____ 9. Under this inventory system, the revenues from sales are recorded when sales are made, but no attempt is made on the sales date to record the cost of the merchandise sold.

_____ 10. Under this inventory system, both the sales amount and the cost of merchandise sold amount are recorded when each item of merchandise is sold.

PART 2

Instructions: Indicate whether each of the following statements is true or false by placing a check mark in the appropriate column.

	True	False
1. A discount offered the purchaser of goods as a means of encouraging payment before the end of the credit period is known as a bank discount	_____	_____
2. Substantial reductions granted to customers by manufacturers and wholesalers of certain types of commodities from the list prices quoted in their catalogs are known as cash discounts	_____	_____
3. Credit terms of "2/10, n/30" mean that the buyer may deduct 2% of the amount of the invoice if payment is made within 10 days of the invoice date	_____	_____
4. If the seller is to absorb the cost of delivering the goods, the terms are stated FOB (free on board) shipping point	_____	_____
5. The two main systems for accounting for merchandise held for sale are called periodic and perpetual	_____	_____
6. The debit balance of the merchandise inventory account appearing in the trial balance represents the amount of the inventory at the end of the current year	_____	_____
7. The balance in the merchandise inventory account at the beginning of the period represents the cost of the merchandise on hand at that time	_____	_____
8. After all necessary adjustments are entered on the work sheet, the two Adjustments columns are totaled to prove the equality of debits and credits	_____	_____
9. Both the debit and credit amounts for Income Summary are extended to the Income Statement columns of the work sheet	_____	_____
10. The difference between the debit and credit columns of the Income Statement section of the work sheet is normally larger than the difference between the debit and credit columns of the Balance Sheet section	_____	_____

PART 3

Instructions: Complete each of the following statements by circling the letter of the best answer.

1. A buyer receives an invoice for $60 dated June 10. If the terms are 2/10, n/30, and the buyer pays the invoice within the discount period, what amount will the seller receive?
   a. $60
   b. $58.80
   c. $48
   d. $1.20

2. The purchases discount account is a contra account to
   a. Accounts Payable
   b. Sales Discounts
   c. Sales
   d. Purchases

3. When a seller of merchandise allows a customer a reduction from the original price for defective goods, the seller usually issues to the customer a(n)
   a. debit memorandum
   b. credit memorandum
   c. sales invoice
   d. inventory slip

4. When the seller prepays the transportation costs and the terms of sale are FOB shipping point, the seller records the payment of the transportation costs by debiting
   a. Accounts Receivable
   b. Sales
   c. Transportation In
   d. Accounts Payable

5. If the seller collects sales tax at the time of sale, the seller credits the tax to
   a. Sales
   b. Accounts Receivable
   c. Sales Tax Payable
   d. Sales Tax Receivable

PART 4

Instructions: Prepare entries for each of the following related transactions of Meuser Co. in the general journal given below.

(1) Purchased $4,000 of merchandise from Willem Co. on account, terms 2/10, n/30.
(2) Paid Willem Co. on account for purchases, less discount.
(3) Purchased $3,000 of merchandise from Arris Co. on account, terms FOB shipping point, 2/10, n/30, with prepaid shipping costs of $80 added to the invoice.
(4) Returned merchandise from Arris Co., $500.
(5) Paid Arris Co. on account for purchases, less returns and discount.

JOURNAL

PAGE

DATE	DESCRIPTION	POST. REF.	DEBIT	CREDIT

PART 5

Instructions: Prepare entries for each of the following related transactions of Perline Co. in the general journal given below.

(1) Sold merchandise for cash, $2,300.
(2) Sold merchandise on nonbank credit cards and reported accounts to the card company, $3,880.
(3) Received cash from card company for nonbank credit card sales, less $175 service fee.
(4) Sold merchandise on account to Trask Co., $4,200, terms 2/10, n/30, FOB shipping point. Prepaid transportation costs of $125 at the customer's request.
(5) Received merchandise returned by Trask Co., $300.
(6) Received cash on account from Trask Co. for sale and transportation costs, less returns and discount.

JOURNAL   PAGE

DATE	DESCRIPTION	POST. REF.	DEBIT	CREDIT

PART 6

Instructions: On the basis of the following data, prepare the cost of goods sold section of the income statement for the fiscal year ended June 30, 1987, for Sylman Co.

Merchandise Inventory, June 30, 1987 . . . . $170,000
Merchandise Inventory, July 1, 1986 145,000
Purchases 480,000
Purchases Returns and Allowances 4,200
Purchases Discounts 5,100
Transportation In 3,300

PART 7

Instructions: Record the following adjustments in the Adjustments columns and complete the work sheet for Gurnee Corporation for the fiscal year ended May 31.

(a) Transfer the beginning inventory to Income Summary.
(b) The merchandise inventory on May 31 is $112,800.
(c) The office supplies on hand May 31 are $980.
(d) The insurance expense for the year is $12,900.
(e) Depreciation on delivery equipment for the year is $8,600.

	ACCOUNT TITLE	TRIAL BALANCE		ADJUSTMENTS	
		DEBIT	CREDIT	DEBIT	CREDIT
1	Cash	7 2 9 0 0 00			
2	Accounts Receivable	11 6 0 0 0 00			
3	Merchandise Inventory	15 6 3 9 0 00			
4	Office Supplies	1 0 2 5 0 00			
5	Prepaid Insurance	2 5 7 4 0 00			
6	Delivery Equipment	6 0 2 0 0 00			
7	Accumulated Depreciation–Delivery Equip.		1 2 9 0 0 00		
8	Accounts Payable		7 7 6 0 0 00		
9	Capital Stock		13 5 0 0 0 00		
10	Retained Earnings		6 0 9 0 0 00		
11	Income Summary				
12	Sales		103 5 7 0 0 00		
13	Sales Returns and Allowances	1 1 0 0 0 00			
14	Purchases	67 1 9 0 0 00			
15	Purchases Discounts		8 3 0 0 00		
16	Sales Salaries Expense	7 8 2 0 0 00			
17	Advertising Expense	1 2 0 9 0 00			
18	Delivery Expense	4 2 0 0 0 00			
19	Depreciation Expense–Delivery Equip.				
20	Miscellaneous Selling Expense	1 3 9 0 0 00			
21	Office Salaries Expense	5 3 4 0 0 00			
22	Office Supplies Expense				
23	Insurance Expense				
24	Miscellaneous General Expense	6 4 3 0 00			
25		133 0 4 0 0 00	133 0 4 0 0 00		
26					
27					
28					
29					
30					
31					
32					
33					
34					
35					
36					
37					
38					
39					
40					
41					
42					

Name _____

Corporation _____

Sheet _____

May 31, 19 _____

ADJUSTED TRIAL BALANCE		INCOME STATEMENT		BALANCE SHEET		
DEBIT	CREDIT	DEBIT	CREDIT	DEBIT	CREDIT	
						1
						2
						3
						4
						5
						6
						7
						8
						9
						10
						11
						12
						13
						14
						15
						16
						17
						18
						19
						20
						21
						22
						23
						24
						25
						26
						27
						28
						29
						30
						31
						32
						33
						34
						35
						36
						37
						38
						39
						40
						41
						42

Page Not Used

Chapter 5

PERIODIC REPORTING FOR A MERCHANDISING ENTERPRISE

STUDY GOALS

After studying this chapter, you should be able to:

1. Summarize the alternative formats and terminology for the income statement, retained earnings statement, and balance sheet of a merchandising enterprise.
2. Prepare an income statement, retained earnings statement, and balance sheet from the work sheet of a merchandising enterprise.
3. Prepare adjusting entries and closing entries for a merchandising enterprise.
4. Prepare reversing entries for a merchandising enterprise.
5. Prepare interim financial statements.
6. Summarize the procedures for correcting errors in accounting records.

GLOSSARY OF KEY TERMS

Account form of balance sheet. A balance sheet with assets on the left-hand side and liabilities and owner's equity on the right-hand side.

Cost of merchandise sold. The cost of the merchandise purchased by a merchandise enterprise and sold.

General expense. Expense incurred in the general operation of a business.

Gross profit. The excess of net revenue from sales over the cost of merchandise sold.

Income from operations. The excess of gross profit over total operating expenses.

Interim statement. A financial statement issued for a period covering less than a fiscal year.

Multiple-step income statement. An income statement with numerous sections and subsections with several intermediate balances before net income.

Net income. The final figure in the income statement when revenues exceed expenses.

Net loss. The final figure in the income statement when expenses exceed revenues.

Other expense. An expense that cannot be associated definitely with operations.

Other income. Revenue from sources other than the principal activity of a business.

Report form of balance sheet. The form of balance sheet with the liability and owner's equity sections presented below the asset section.

Retained earnings statement. A statement for a corporate enterprise, summarizing the changes in retained earnings during a specific period of time.

Reversing entry. An entry that reverses a specific adjusting entry to facilitate the recording of routine transactions in the subsequent period.

Selling expense. An expense incurred directly and entirely in connection with the sale of merchandise.

Single-step income statement. An income statement with the total of all expenses deducted from the total of all revenues.

CHAPTER OUTLINE

I. Financial Statements for Merchandising Enterprises.
   A. The basic financial statements for a merchandising enterprise are similar to those of a service enterprise, except for the following:

    1. For a corporate enterprise, the financial statements would include the retained earnings statement rather than the statement of owner's equity.
    2. For a merchandising enterprise, the in-

come statement includes a cost of merchandise sold section. This section was described in Chapter 4.

    3. For a merchandising enterprise, the balance sheet includes merchandise inventory as a current asset.

B. The multiple-step income statement contains many sections, subsections, and intermediate balances.

    1. The total of all charges to customers for merchandise sold, both for cash and on account, is reported as revenue from sales. Sales returns and allowances and sales discounts are deducted from the gross sales amount to yield net sales.

    2. The cost of merchandise sold section appears next, as described and illustrated in Chapter 4.

    3. The excess of the net revenue from sales over the cost of merchandise sold is called gross profit.

    4. Operating expenses are generally grouped into selling expenses and general expenses or administrative expenses.

    5. The excess of gross profit over total operating expenses is called income from operations, or operating income. If operating expenses are greater than gross profit, the excess is loss from operations.

    6. Revenue from sources other than the principal activity of a business is classified as other income. In a merchandising enterprise, this category often includes income from interest, rent, dividends, and gains resulting from the sale of plant assets.

    7. Expenses that cannot be associated definitely with operations are identified as other expense, or nonoperating expense. Interest expense and losses incurred in the disposal of plant assets are examples of items that are reported in this section.

    8. The final figure on the income statement is labeled net income (or net loss).

C. The single-step form of income statement derives its name from the fact that the total of all expenses is deducted from all revenues.

D. The retained earnings statement summarizes the changes which have occurred in the retained earnings account during the fiscal period.

    1. The retained earnings statement is the connecting link between the income statement and the balance sheet.

    2. It is not unusual to add the analysis of retained earnings at the bottom of the income statement to form a combined income and retained earnings statement.

E. The balance sheet is the last financial statement usually prepared for a merchandising enterprise.

    1. The arrangement of the assets on the left-hand side of the balance sheet, with liabilities and owner's equity on the right-hand side, is referred to as the account form of balance sheet.

    2. When the balance sheet is prepared in downward sequence, with total assets equaling the combined totals of liabilities and owner's equity, it is referred to as the report form.

II. Adjusting Entries.

A. The analyses necessary to prepare the adjusting entries are completed during the process of preparing the work sheet. Therefore, it is only necessary to refer to the work sheet when recording the adjusting entries in the journal.

B. After the adjusting entries are posted, the balances of all asset, liability, revenue, and expense accounts should correspond exactly to the amounts reported in the financial statements.

III. Closing Entries.

A. Closing entries are recorded in the journal immediately following the adjusting entries and reduce all temporary owner's equity accounts to zero balances. The final effect of closing out such balances is a net increase or net decrease in the retained earnings account.

B. The four entries required to close the accounts of a corporation are as follows:

    1. The first entry closes all income statement accounts with credit balances by transferring the total to the credit side of Income Summary.

    2. The second entry closes all income statement accounts with debit balances by transferring the total to the debit side of Income Summary.

    3. The third entry closes Income Summary by transferring its balance, the net income or net loss for the year, to Retained Earnings.

    4. The fourth entry closes Dividends by transferring its balance to Retained Earnings.

C. After all temporary owner's equity accounts have been closed, the only accounts with balances are the asset, contra asset, liability, capital stock, and retained earnings accounts. Balances of these accounts in the ledger will correspond exactly with the amounts reported on the balance sheet.

IV. Post-Closing Trial Balance.

A. After the adjusting and closing entries have been recorded, it is advisable to take another trial balance to verify the debit-credit equality of the ledger at the beginning of the following year.

B. The trial balance taken after the adjusting and closing entries have been recorded is called the post-closing trial balance.

V. Reversing Entries.

A. Some of the adjusting entries recorded at the end of the fiscal year have an important effect on transactions that occur in the following year.

B. Reversing entries are an optional procedure which exactly reverses adjusting entries made at the end of a preceding fiscal period. This process simplifies the recording of otherwise routine transactions that occur in the subsequent period.

VI. Interim Statements.

A. Financial statements issued for periods covering less than a fiscal year are called interim statements.

B. When interim financial statements are prepared, the adjustment data are assembled and a work sheet is completed as of the end of the interim period. Although the work sheet serves as a basis for preparing interim state-

ments, adjusting and closing entries are recorded only at the end of the fiscal period.

C. The amounts of the asset and liability accounts appearing in the balance sheet section of the work sheet for an interim period are the balances as of the last day of that period.

D. The income statement data for an interim period are obtained by subtracting from the amount of each revenue and expense of the current cumulative income statement the corresponding amount from the preceding cumulative income statement period.

VII. Correction of Errors.

A. Occasional errors in journalizing and posting transactions are unavoidable. Procedures used to correct errors in the journal and ledger vary according to the nature of the error and the phase of the accounting cycle in which it is discovered.

B. The procedures for correction of errors are summarized in the following table:

Error	Correction Procedure
Journal entry incorrect, but not posted.	Draw line through the error and insert correct title or amount.
Journal entry correct, but posted incorrectly.	Draw line through the error and post correctly.
Journal entry incorrect and posted.	Journalize and post a correcting entry.

PART 1

Instructions: A list of terms and related statements appear below. From the list of terms, select the one that relates to each statement and print its identifying letter in the space provided.

A. Account form
B. General expenses
C. Gross profit
D. Income from operations

E. Interim statements
F. Multiple-step
G. Other expense

H. Report form
I. Selling expenses
J. Single-step

_____ 1. The form of income statement that has many sections, subsections, and intermediate balances.

_____ 2. The form of income statement in which the total of all expenses is deducted from the total of all revenues.

_____ 3. The excess of the net revenue from sales over the cost of merchandise sold.

_____ 4. Expenses that are incurred directly and entirely in connection with the sale of merchandise are classified as (?)

_____ 5. Expenses incurred in the general operations of the business are classified as (?)

_____ 6. The excess of gross profit over total operating expenses is called (?)

_____ 7. Expenses that cannot be associated definitely with operations are identified as (?)

_____ 8. The form of balance sheet with the assets on the left-hand side and the liabilities and owner's equity on the right-hand side is referred to as the (?)

_____ 9. The form of balance sheet in which the liabilities and owner's equity sections are listed below rather than to the right of the asset section is referred to as the (?)

_____ 10. Financial statements issued for periods covering less than a fiscal year are called (?)

PART 2

Instructions: Indicate whether each of the following statements is true or false by placing a check mark in the appropriate column.

	True	False

1. Expenses incurred directly and entirely in connection with the sale of merchandise are called general or administrative expenses. . . . .   ____ ____

2. Revenue from sources such as income from interest, rent, dividends, and gains resulting from the sale of plant assets is classified as income from operations. . . . .   ____ ____

3. The single-step form of income statement has the advantage of being simple and it emphasizes total revenues and total expenses as the factors that determine net income. . . . .   ____ ____

4. Gross profit is not calculated in the single-step form of income statement. . . . .   ____ ____

5. The excess of gross profit over total operating expenses is called income from operations. . . . . . .   ____ ____

6. The traditional balance sheet arrangement of assets on the left-hand side, with the liabilities and owner's equity on the right-hand side, is called the report form. . . . .   ____ ____

7. After the adjusting and closing entries have been recorded and posted, the general ledger accounts that appear on the balance sheet have no balances. . . . .   ____ ____

8. In a reversing entry, the accounts and the corresponding amounts in the related adjusting entry are reversed. . . . .   ____ ____

9. After the reversing entry for accrued salary expense is posted and the first payroll for January has been posted, the balance of the salary expense account automatically represents the current expense of the new period. . . . .   ____ ____

10. When interim financial statements are to be prepared, the adjustment data are assembled and a work sheet is completed as of the end of the interim period, but adjusting and closing entries are not recorded in the accounts. . . . .   ____ ____

PART 3

Instructions: Complete each of the following statements by circling the letter of the best answer.

1. The basic differences between the financial statements of a merchandising enterprise and a service enterprise include the cost of merchandise sold section of the income statement and the

   a. owner's equity section of the balance sheet
   b. other income section of the income statement
   c. inclusion of merchandise inventory on the balance sheet as a current asset
   d. inclusion of a retained earnings statement

2. The excess of net revenue from sales over the cost of merchandise sold is called
   a. gross profit
   b. operating profit
   c. net profit from operations
   d. merchandising income

3. Income from operations is computed by subtracting from gross profit the
   a. selling expenses
   b. general expenses
   c. total administrative expenses
   d. total operating expenses

4. After all adjusting entries are posted, the balances of all asset, liability, revenue, and expense accounts correspond exactly to the amounts in the
   a. work sheet trial balance
   b. general journal
   c. post-closing trial balance
   d. financial statements

5. When an erroneous journal entry has been made and the error is not discovered until after posting is completed, the appropriate correction procedure is to
   a. erase the entry, posting, and any subsequent postings affecting the account balances, and make the correct entries
   b. journalize and post a correcting entry
   c. draw a line through the journal entry error and insert the correct account or amount
   d. draw a line through the posting error and insert the correct account or amount

PART 4

Karl Co. closes its books each year on December 31. On December 31 of the current year, the salary expense account has a debit balance of $48,500. Karl's last regular payday was Friday, December 28, for the preceding week. Karl Co. owes its employees $260 for working Monday, December 31.

Instructions: Record the following entries in the general journal and post to the general ledger accounts below and on the following page:

(1) the adjusting entry for salaries payable as of December 31.
(2) The closing entry to close the salary expense account to Income Summary.
(3) The reversing entry for salaries payable as of January 1 of the following year.
(4) The entry to record the payroll for the week ended January 4 of the following year. Salaries totaled $1,300 for the week.

JOURNAL   PAGE 23

DATE	DESCRIPTION	POST. REF.	DEBIT	CREDIT

ACCOUNT   Salaries Payable   ACCOUNT NO.   213

DATE	ITEM	POST. REF.	DEBIT	CREDIT	BALANCE DEBIT	BALANCE CREDIT

ACCOUNT   Income Summary   ACCOUNT NO.   313

DATE	ITEM	POST. REF.	DEBIT	CREDIT	BALANCE DEBIT	BALANCE CREDIT

DATE		ITEM	POST. REF.	DEBIT	CREDIT	BALANCE	
						DEBIT	CREDIT
19--Dec.	31	Balance				4 8 5 0 0	

PART 5

Instructions: Use the work sheet in Part 7 of Chapter 4 for this problem.

(1) Record the adjusting entries in the general journal below.

JOURNAL

PAGE _____

DATE	DESCRIPTION	POST. REF.	DEBIT	CREDIT

(2) Record the closing entries in the general journal below.

DATE	DESCRIPTION	POST. REF.	DEBIT	CREDIT

Chapter 5

Name _____

PART 6

Instructions: Using the Income Statement columns of the work sheet in Part 7 of Chapter 4, prepare a multiple-step income statement with a cost of goods sold section for the year ended May 31, 19—.

Gurnee Corporation
Income Statement
For Year Ended May 31, 19—

PART 7

Instructions: Use the Balance Sheet columns of the work sheet in Part 7 of Chapter 4 for this problem.

(1) Prepare a balance sheet in report form as of May 31, 19—.

Gurnee Corporation
Balance Sheet
May 31, 19—

(2) Prepare a post-closing trial balance as of May 31, 19—. Note that the figure shown on the work sheet for Retained Earnings must be increased by the amount of the net income for the year.

Gurnee Corporation
Post-Closing Trial Balance
May 31, 19—

Page not used

Chapter 6

DEFERRALS AND ACCRUALS

STUDY GOALS

After studying this chapter, you should be able to:
1. List the common classifications of deferrals and accruals.
2. Prepare journal entries for the two alternative systems for accounting for prepaid expenses (deferrals).
3. Prepare journal entries for the two alternative systems for accounting for unearned revenues (deferrals).
4. Prepare the journal entries for accrued liabilities (accrued expenses).
5. Prepare journal entries for accrued assets (accrued revenues).

GLOSSARY OF KEY TERMS

Accrual. An expense or a revenue that gradually increases with the passage of time.

Accrued asset (accrued revenue) or accrued liability (accrued expense). An asset (revenue) or a liability (expense) that gradually increases with the passage of time and that is recorded at the end of the accounting period by an adjusting entry.

Deferral. A postponement of the recognition of an expense already paid or a revenue already received.

Prepaid expense. A purchased commodity or service that has not been consumed at the end of an accounting period.

Reversing entry. An entry that reverses a specific adjusting entry to facilitate the recording of routine transactions in the subsequent period.

Unearned revenue. Revenue received in advance of its being earned.

CHAPTER OUTLINE

I. Classification and Terminology.
  A. Every adjusting entry affects both a balance sheet account and income statement account. In no case will an adjusting entry affect only an asset and a liability (both balance sheet) or only an expense and a revenue (both income statement) accounts.
  B. A deferral is a delay of recognition of an expense already paid or a revenue already received.
    1. Deferred expenses expected to benefit a short period of time are listed on the balance sheet among the current assets, as prepaid expenses.
    2. Deferred expenses which represent long-term prepayments are presented on the balance sheet in the section called deferred charges.
    3. Deferred revenues expected to be earned in a short period of time may be listed on the balance sheet as current liabilities, where they are called unearned revenues or revenues received in advance.
    4. If a long period of time is involved, deferred revenues are presented on the balance sheet in the section called deferred credits.
  C. An accrual is an expense that has not been paid or a revenue that has not been received.
    1. Accrued expenses are described in the balance sheet as accrued liabilities, and since they are ordinarily due within a year, they are listed as current liabilities.
    2. Accrued revenues are listed on the balance sheet as accrued assets, and since they are usually due within a short time, they are classified as current assets.
II. Prepaid Expenses (Deferrals).
  A. Prepaid expenses are the costs of goods and services that have been purchased but not used at the end of the accounting period.
  B. At the time the expense is prepaid, it may be recorded initially as an asset.
    1. The amount of the prepaid expense actually used is determined at the end of the accounting period.
    2. An adjusting entry at the end of the ac-

counting period debits an expense account and credits the asset account for the amount of the adjustment.

   3. There is no reversing entry made at the end of the period for prepaid expenses recorded in this manner.

  C. At the time an expense is prepaid, it may be recorded initially as an expense.

   1. The amount of the expense actually unused is then determined at the end of the accounting period.

   2. The accounts are adjusted by debiting the asset account and crediting the expense account for the amount of the adjustment.

   3. When prepaid expenses are recorded in this manner, a reversing entry is made as of the first day of the subsequent accounting period. This entry is the exact reverse of the adjusting entry made at the end of the preceding accounting period. In this manner, the recording of future transactions may continue to be made in the routine manner of debiting an expense account at the time of the expenditure.

  D. Although the journal entries for the two systems of recording prepaid expenses differ, both methods will yield the same account balances as of the end of the accounting period. Either of the two systems may be used for all the prepaid expenses of the enterprise, or one system may be used for prepayment of some kinds of expenses and the other system for other kinds.

  E. Initially debiting an asset account is logical for prepayments of a long-term nature, while initially debiting an expense account is logical for prepayments of a short-term nature.

  F. The system adopted by an enterprise for each kind of prepaid expense should be followed consistently from year to year.

III. Unearned Revenues (Deferrals).

  A. Items of revenue that are received in advance represent a liability that may be termed unearned revenue. Examples of such revenue include subscriptions received by magazine publishers, prepaid rent, and premiums received on insurance policies.

  B. When revenue is received in advance, it may be credited to a liability account.

   1. At the end of the accounting period, the amount of the revenue that has been earned must be determined.

   2. That portion of the revenue that has been earned must be adjusted by debiting the liability account and crediting the revenue account.

  C. When revenue is received in advance, it may be credited to a revenue account as the cash is received.

   1. At the end of the accounting period, the amount of the revenue that has not been earned must be recorded as a liability.

   2. The amount of unearned revenue is adjusted at the end of the accounting period by debiting the revenue account and crediting the liability account.

   3. To facilitate the recording of transactions in subsequent periods, a reversing entry is made as of the first day of the subsequent accounting period.

  D. The amounts reported as revenues on the income statement and as liabilities on the balance sheet will not be affected by which of the two systems is used. To avoid confusion the system used should be followed consistently from year to year.

IV. Accrued Liabilities (Accrued Expenses).

  A. Expenses that accrue from day to day but are recorded only when they are paid are called accrued liabilities or accrued expenses.

  B. The adjusting entry for an accrued liability is to debit an expense account and to credit a liability account.

  C. Reversing entries are usually made for adjustments of accrued liabilities.

V. Accrued Assets (Accrued Revenues).

  A. Some assets accrue from day to day but are usually recorded only when cash is received. Such assets are called accrued assets or accrued revenues.

  B. An adjusting entry must be made at the end of the accounting period for all accrued assets that have not been recorded. This entry debits an asset account and credits an associated revenue account.

  C. Reversing entries are usually made for adjustments of accrued assets.

VI. Summary of Use of Reversing Entries.

  A. The use of reversing entries is an optional procedure designed to simplify the recording of routine transactions.

  B. Reversing entries are normally prepared for adjusting entries related to the following types of transactions:

   1. When a prepaid expense has been initially recorded as an expense;

   2. When an unearned revenue has been initially recorded as a revenue;

   3. When an accrued liability has been recorded;

   4. When an accrued asset has been recorded.

PART 1

Instructions: A list of terms and related statements appear below. From the list of terms, select the one that relates to each statement and print its identifying letter in the space provided.

A. Accrual   **E.** Deferral   **H.** Revenue
B. Accrued assets   **F.** Expense   **I.** Revenue account
C. Accrued liabilities   **G.** Prepaid expenses   **J.** Unearned revenues
D. Asset account

_____ 1. A delay of the recognition of an expense already paid or of a revenue already received.

_____ 2. Deferred expenses expected to benefit a short period of time are listed on the balance sheet among the current assets, and are called (?)

_____ 3. Deferred revenues may be listed on the balance sheet as a current liability, where they are called revenues received in advance, or (?)

_____ 4. An expense that has not been paid or a revenue that has not been received is called a(n) (?)

_____ 5. Accrued expenses may also be described on the balance sheet as (?)

_____ 6. Accrued revenues may also be described on the balance sheet as (?)

_____ 7. At the time an expense is prepaid, it may be debited to either an expense account or a(n) (?)

_____ 8. As cash is received, instead of being credited to a liability account, unearned revenue may be credited to a(n) (?)

_____ 9. A reversing entry should be prepared when a prepaid expense has been initially recorded as a(n) (?)

_____ 10. A reversing entry should be prepared when an unearned revenue has been initially recorded as a(n) (?)

PART 2

Instructions: Indicate whether each of the following statements is true or false by placing a check mark in the appropriate column.

	True	False
1. Every adjusting entry affects both a balance sheet account and an income statement account	_____	_____
2. Long-term prepayments that can be charged to operations of several years are called deferred charges	_____	_____
3. A deferral is an expense that has not been paid or a revenue that has not been received	_____	_____
4. Accrued expenses may be described on the balance sheet as accrued liabilities	_____	_____
5. At the time that an expense is prepaid, it may be debited to either an asset account or a liability account	_____	_____
6. If a prepaid expense is recorded initially as an expense, an adjusting entry is used to transfer the unused amount to an appropriate liability account	_____	_____
7. The effect of the reversing entry for a prepayment is to transfer the entire balance of an asset account to an expense account immediately after the temporary accounts have been closed for the period	_____	_____
8. A reversing entry is not required if a prepaid expense is recorded initially as an expense	_____	_____
9. Either of the two suggested systems for recording revenues received in advance may be used, as long as the system adopted for each type of revenue is followed consistently from year to year ...	_____	_____
10. The amount of accrued revenue is recorded by debiting a liability account and crediting a revenue account	_____	_____

PART 3

Instructions: Complete each of the following statements by circling the letter of the best answer.

1. A delay of the recognition of an expense already paid or a revenue already received is known as a(n)
   a. deferral
   b. adjustment
   c. accrual
   d. postponement

2. Deferred expenses expected to benefit a short period of time are called
   a. deferred charges
   b. prepaid expenses
   c. deferred costs
   d. accrued liabilities

3. Deferred revenues which involve a long period of time are presented on the balance sheet in a section called
   a. deferred charges
   b. revenue liabilities
   c. accrued receivables
   d. deferred credits

4. Accrued revenues may be described on the balance sheet as
   a. accrued liabilities
   b. accrued credits
   c. accrued assets
   d. estimated accruals

5. If a prepaid expense is recorded initially as an asset, an adjusting entry is used to transfer the amount used to an appropriate
   a. liability account
   b. expense account
   c. deferral account
   d. accrual account

6. Items of revenue that are received in advance represent a liability that may be termed
   a. accrued revenue
   b. accrued liability
   c. deferred assets
   d. unearned revenue

7. When revenue is received in advance, it may be credited to either a liability or a(n)
   a. revenue account
   b. asset account
   c. expense account
   d. capital account

8. If unearned revenue is recorded initially as a liability, an adjusting entry is used to transfer the amount earned to an appropriate
   a. asset account
   b. current liability account
   c. accrual account
   d. revenue account

9. A reversing entry is not required if unearned revenue is recorded initially as a(n)
   a. asset
   b. expense
   c. liability
   d. revenue

10. The amounts of accrued but unpaid expenses at the end of the fiscal period are both an expense and a(n)
    a. liability
    b. asset
    c. deferral
    d. revenue

PART 4

Campbell Co.'s prepaid insurance account has a balance of $5,100 at the end of the current year (before adjustment). This amount represents unexpired insurance at the beginning of the year plus the total of the premiums on policies purchased during the year. Campbell's insurance records show that $3,850 of insurance premiums have expired during the year.

Instructions: (1) Record the adjusting entry (without explanation) as of December 31 and post to the T accounts below.

(2) Record the closing entry (without explanation) as of December 31 and post to the T accounts. Establish the new balance in the prepaid insurance account and rule the insurance expense account.

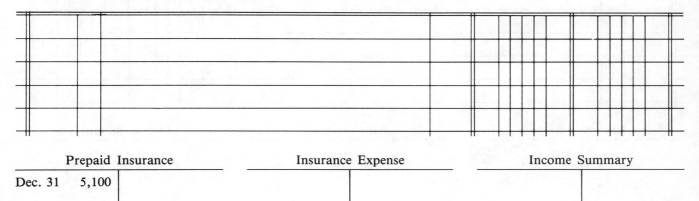

	Prepaid Insurance		Insurance Expense		Income Summary
Dec. 31 5,100					

PART 5

Snyder Co.'s rent expense account has a balance of $6,200 at the end of the current year. As of December 31, $3,800 of this balance has become an expense of the current year.

Instructions: (1) Record the adjusting entry (without explanation) as of December 31 and post to the T accounts below.

(2) Record the closing entry (without explanation) as of December 31 and post to the T accounts. Rule the expense account.

(3) Record the reversing entry (without explanation) as of January 1 of the next year and post to the T accounts. Rule the prepaid rent account.

	Prepaid Rent		Rent Expense		Income Summary
			Dec. 31 6,200		

PART 6

Stewart Co.'s unearned rent account has a balance of $36,000 at December 31 of the current year. This amount represents the rental of an apartment for a period of three years. The lease began on October 1 of the current year.

Instructions: (1) Record the adjusting entry (without explanation) as of December 31 and post to the T accounts below.

(2) Record the closing entry (without explanation) as of December 31 and post to the T accounts. Establish the new balance in the unearned rent account. Rule the rent income amount.

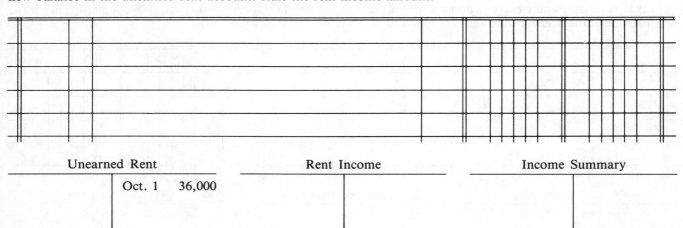

Unearned Rent	Rent Income	Income Summary
Oct. 1 36,000		

PART 7

Griswold Co.'s rent income account has a balance of $84,000 at December 31 of the current year. This amount represents the rental of space in a warehouse for a period of four years. The lease began on May 1 of the current year.

Instructions: (1) Record the adjusting entry (without explanation) as of December 31 and post to the T accounts below.

(2) Record the closing entry (without explanation) as of December 31 and post to the T accounts. Rule the rent income account.

(3) Record the reversing entry (without explanation) as of January 1 of the next year and post to the T accounts. Rule the unearned rent account.

Unearned Rent	Rent Income	Income Summary
	May 1 84,000	

PART 8

Goodman Inc.'s salary expense account has a balance of $84,000 at the end of the current year, representing salaries paid in cash through Saturday, December 29. Salaries accrued through December 31 amount to $1,250.

Instructions: (1) Record the adjusting entry (without explanation) as of December 31 and post to the T accounts below.
(2) Record the closing entry (without explanation) as of December 31 and post to the T accounts. Rule the closed account.
(3) Record the reversing entry (without explanation) as of January 1 of the next year and post to the T accounts. Rule the appropriate account.

Salaries Payable	Salary Expense	Income Summary
	Dec. 31 84,000	

PART 9

Daniels Co.'s delivery service income account has a balance of $3,200 at the end of the current year, representing cash collections for services performed during the year. The unbilled services at December 31 total $900.

Instructions: (1) Record the adjusting entry (without explanation) as of December 31 and post to the T accounts below.

(2) Record the closing entry (without explanation) as of December 31 and post to the T accounts. Rule the closed account.

(3) Record the reversing entry (without explanation) as of January 1 of the next year and post to the T accounts. Rule the appropriate account.

Delivery Service Receivable

Delivery Service Income

Dec. 31 3,200

Income Summary

Chapter 7   ACCOUNTING SYSTEMS DESIGN

After studying this chapter, you should be able to:
1. List the principles of properly designed accounting systems.
2. Summarize the three phases of accounting system installation and revision.
3. List the principles of internal control.
4. Explain how data processing methods may be used in accounting systems.
5. Use the following special journals to record transactions:

    Purchases journal
    Cash payments journal
    Sales journal
    Cash receipts journal
6. Use subsidiary ledgers in recording transactions.
7. Explain how electronic data processing (EDP) systems may be used to process accounting data.

GLOSSARY OF KEY TERMS

Accounting system. The system that provides the information for use in conducting the affairs of the business and reporting to owners, creditors, and other interested parties.

Accounts payable ledger. The subsidiary ledger containing the individual accounts with suppliers (creditors).

Accounts receivable ledger. The subsidiary ledger containing the individual accounts with customers (debtors).

Cash payments journal. The journal in which all cash payments are recorded.

Cash receipts journal. The journal in which all cash receipts are recorded.

Controlling account. The account in the general ledger that summarizes the balances of a subsidiary ledger.

Electronic data processing (EDP). The term applied to the processing of data by electronic equipment.

General journal. The two-column form used to record journal entries that do not "fit" in any special journals.

General ledger. The principal ledger, when used in conjunction with subsidiary ledgers, that contains all of the balance sheet and income statement accounts.

Internal accounting controls. Procedures and records that are mainly concerned with the reliability of financial records and reports and with the safeguarding of assets.

Internal administrative controls. Procedures and records that aid management in achieving business goals.

Internal controls. The detailed procedures adopted by an enterprise to control its operations.

Purchases journal. The journal in which all items purchased on account are recorded.

Sales journal. The journal in which all sales of merchandise on account are recorded.

Special journal. A journal designed to record a single type of transaction.

Subsidiary ledger. A ledger containing individual accounts with a common characteristic.

CHAPTER OUTLINE

I. Principles of Accounting Systems.
   A. Although accounting systems vary from business to business, a number of broad principles apply to all systems.
   B. Although an accounting system must be tailored to meet the specific needs of each business, reports should not be produced if the cost of the report is more than the benefit received by those who use it (cost-effectiveness balance).
   C. An accounting system must be flexible enough to meet future needs of the business

as the environment in which it operates changes (flexibility to meet future needs).

D. The detailed procedures inherent in an accounting system to control operations are called internal controls (adequate internal controls).

E. An accounting system must provide effective reports in an understandable manner (effective reporting).

F. Only by effectively using and adapting to the human resources of the business can the accounting system meet information needs at the lowest cost (adaptation to organizational structure).

II. Accounting System Installation and Revision.

A. Many large businesses continually review their accounting system and may constantly be involved in changing some part of it.

B. Systems analysis is one phase of accounting system installation and revision. The goal of systems analysis is to determine information needs, the sources of such information, and the deficiencies in procedures and data processing methods presently used.

C. Systems design is a second phase of accounting system installation and revision. Systems designers must have a general knowledge of the qualities of different kinds of data processing equipment, and the ability to evaluate alternatives.

D. The final phase of the creation or revision of an accounting system is to carry out, or implement, the proposals. In the systems implementation phase, all personnel responsible for operating the system must be carefully trained and closely supervised until satisfactory efficiency is achieved.

III. Internal Controls.

A. Internal controls are classified as (1) administrative controls and (2) accounting controls.

1. Internal administrative controls consist of procedures and records that aid management in achieving business goals.

2. Internal accounting controls consist of procedures and records that are mainly concerned with the reliability of financial records and reports and with the safeguarding of assets.

B. Details of a system of internal control will vary according to the size and type of business enterprise.

C. Several broad principles of internal control include the following:

1. The successful operation of an accounting system requires competent personnel who are able to perform the duties to which they are assigned. In addition, rotation of duties is also very helpful in disclosing any irregularities that may have occurred (competent personnel and

rotation of duties).

2. If employees are to work efficiently, their responsibilities must be clearly defined and assigned (assignment of responsibility).

3. To decrease the possibility of inefficiency, errors, and fraud, responsibility for a sequence of related operations should be divided among two or more persons (separation of responsibility for related operations).

4. Responsibility for maintaining the accounting records should be separated from the responsibility for engaging in business transactions and for the custody of a firm's assets (separation of operations and accounting).

5. Proofs and security measures such as the use of cash registers and fidelity insurance should be used to safeguard business assets and assure reliable accounting data (proofs and security measures).

6. To determine whether the other internal control principles are being effectively applied, the system should be periodically reviewed and evaluated by internal auditors (independent review).

IV. Data Processing Methods.

A. The entire amount of data needed by an enterprise is called its data base.

B. Depending upon the variety and the amount of data included in the data base, either a manual or computerized processing method may be used.

C. Whether the accounting system used is either manual or computerized, the basic principles of accounting systems discussed previously are applicable.

V. Subsidiary Ledgers and Special Journals.

A. When there are a large number of individual accounts with a common characteristic, it is common to place them in a separate ledger called a subsidiary ledger. The principal ledger, which contains all the balance sheet and income statement accounts, is then called the general ledger.

B. Each subsidiary ledger is represented by a summarizing account in the general ledger called a controlling account. The sum of the balances of the accounts in a subsidiary ledger must agree with the balance of the related controlling account.

C. The individual accounts with creditors are arranged in alphabetical order in a subsidiary ledger called the accounts payable ledger or creditors ledger. The related controlling account in the general ledger is Accounts Payable.

D. The subsidiary ledger containing the individual accounts for credit customers is called the accounts receivable ledger or customers ledger. The related controlling account in the general ledger is Accounts Receivable.

E. One of the simplest methods of processing data more efficiently in a manual accounting system is to expand the two-column journal to a multicolumn journal. Each amount column included in a multicolumn journal is restricted to the recording of transactions affecting a certain account. Such journals are known as special journals. The two-column journal form used in previous chapters is known as the general journal or simply the journal.

F. The special journals most commonly found in business are as follows:

1. The purchases journal is designed to allow for the recording of all purchases on account. Special columns in the purchases journal include the accounts payable credit column, purchases debit column, store supplies debit column, office supplies debit column, and a sundry (or miscellaneous) accounts debit column.

   a. The individual credits to accounts payable in the purchases journal are posted as the transactions occur.

   b. The totals of the special columns are posted to the individual ledger accounts on a periodic basis, usually at the end of each month.

   c. Purchases returns and allowances are recorded in the normal two-column general journal, as illustrated in Chapter 4.

2. The cash payments journal is designed to record all cash payments. The special columns of the cash payments journal normally include the sundry (or miscellaneous) accounts debit column, accounts payable debit column, purchases discounts credit column, and cash credit column.

   a. Debits to the accounts payable subsidiary ledger are normally posted as the transactions occur.

   b. Periodically the columns of the cash payments journal are totaled and posted to the accounts in the general ledger.

3. The sales journal is used for recording all sales of merchandise on account. The sales journal normally has one column for debiting Accounts Receivable and crediting Sales.

   a. As sales on account occur and are entered in the sales journal, the debits to Accounts Receivable are posted to the subsidiary ledger.

   b. Periodically the column of the sales journal is totaled and posted to the general ledger accounts for Accounts Receivable and Sales.

   c. Sales returns and allowances are recorded in the two-column general journal as illustrated in Chapter 4.

4. All transactions involving cash receipts are recorded in a cash receipts journal. The special columns of the cash receipts journal normally include a sundry (or miscellaneous) accounts credit column, a sales credit column, an accounts receivable credit column, a sales discounts debit column, and a cash debit column.

   a. As cash is received from customers on account, the accounts receivable subsidiary ledger is posted to the individual accounts.

   b. Periodically, the columns of the cash receipts journal are totaled and posted to the general ledger accounts.

VI. Electronic Data Processing Systems.

A. A system that uses an electronic computer to process accounting data is termed an electronic data processing (EDP) system.

B. An EDP system processes accounting data in much the same way as does a manual system but with greater speed and accuracy.

C. In recent years, microcomputers and minicomputers have made EDP processing affordable to small and medium-sized businesses.

PART 1

Instructions: A list of terms and related statements appear below. From the list of terms, select the one that relates to each statement and print its identifying letter in the space provided.

A. Accounts payable ledger   E. General ledger   H. Internal controls
B. Accounts receivable ledger   F. Internal accounting controls   I. Sales journal
C. Cash receipts journal   G. Internal administrative controls   J. Subsidiary ledger
D. Controlling account

_____ 1. The detailed procedures used by management to control operations.

_____ 2. Controls that consist of procedures and records that aid management in the achievement of business goals.

_____ 3. Procedures and records that are mainly concerned with the reliability of financial records and reports and with the safeguarding of assets.

_____ 4. A supplementary record used to provide detailed information for a control account in the general ledger.

_____ 5. The principal ledger, containing all of the balance sheet and income statement accounts.

_____ 6. A general ledger account which is supported by information in a subsidiary ledger.

_____ 7. A subsidiary ledger containing an account with each creditor.

_____ 8. A subsidiary ledger containing an account with each credit customer.

_____ 9. A special journal used exclusively for recording sales of merchandise on account.

_____ 10. A special journal used to record all cash inflows.

PART 2

Instructions: Indicate whether each of the following statements is true or false by placing a check mark in the appropriate column.

	True	False

1. The goal of systems design is to determine information needs, the sources of such information, and the deficiencies in procedures and data processing methods presently used . . . . _____ _____

2. Responsibility for maintaining the accounting records should be separated from the responsibility for custody of the firm's assets . . . . _____ _____

3. Transactions involving the payment of cash for any purpose usually are recorded in a cash journal . . . . _____ _____

4. When there are a large number of individual accounts with a common characteristic, it is common to place them in a separate ledger called a detail ledger . . . . _____ _____

5. For each transaction recorded in the purchases journal, the credit is entered in the column entitled Accounts Payable Cr. . . . . _____ _____

6. Acquisitions on account which are not provided for in special debit columns are recorded in the purchases journal in the final set of columns called Misc. . . . . _____ _____

7. Debits to creditors accounts for invoices paid are recorded in the Accounts Payable Dr. column of the cash payments journal . . . . _____ _____

8. At the end of the month, the total of the amount column of the sales journal is posted as a debit to Cash and a credit to Sales . . . . _____ _____

9. Each amount in the Sundry Accounts Cr. column of the cash receipts journal must be posted individually to an appropriate general ledger account . . . . _____ _____

10. An EDP system processes accounting data in much the same way as does a manual system but with greater speed and accuracy . . . . _____ _____

Instructions: Complete each of the following statements by circling the letter of the best answer.

1. The job of installing or changing an accounting system is made up of three phases: (1) analysis, (2) design, and (3)
   a. installation
   b. verification
   c. management
   d. implementation

2. To determine whether internal control principles are being effectively applied, the system should be periodically reviewed and evaluated by the
   a. users of the system
   b. internal auditors
   c. employees responsible for operations
   d. EDP service center

3. A journal designed especially for the recording of purchases of merchandise or other items on account is called a(n)
   a. purchases journal
   b. credit journal
   c. payments journal
   d. cash payments journal

4. The individual amounts in the Accounts Payable Cr. column of the purchases journal are posted to the appropriate account in the
   a. general ledger
   b. general journal
   c. accounts payable ledger
   d. accounts payable journal

5. When merchandise is returned or a price adjustment is granted, an entry is made in the
   a. general journal
   b. cash receipts journal
   c. adjustments journal
   d. purchases journal

PART 4

During November of the current year, Bluebaum's, a retail store, completed the following transactions with creditors on account:

Nov. 4.   Purchase on account from Peterson Co., $5,300.
     13.   Purchase on account from Quick Corp., $1,150.
     22.   Purchase on account from Gudorf Co., $1,850.
     26.   Purchase on account from Norris Inc., $4,300.

Instructions: (1) Record the above transactions in the single-column purchases journal below.

(2) Post the individual items from the purchases journal to the T accounts. Indicate that each item has been posted by placing a check mark (✓) in the Post. Ref. column of the purchases journal.

(3) Post the total of the purchases journal to the T accounts for Accounts Payable and Purchases. Indicate that the posting is completed by inserting the appropriate account numbers in the journal under the amount posted.

PURCHASES JOURNAL   PAGE 21

DATE	ACCOUNT CREDITED	POST. REF.	PURCHASES, DR. ACCTS. PAY. CR.

GENERAL LEDGER   ACCOUNTS PAYABLE LEDGER

ACCOUNTS PAYABLE   211   Gudorf Co.   Norris Inc.

PURCHASES   511   Peterson Co.   Quick Corp.

(4) Determine that the sum of the balances of the individual accounts in the subsidiary accounts payable ledger agrees with the balance of the accounts payable controlling account in the general ledger by completing the following summary form:

Gudorf Co. .... $ _____

Norris Inc. .... _____

Peterson Co. .... _____

Quick Corp. .... _____

Total accounts payable .... $ _____

PART 5

The following transactions related to purchases and cash payments were completed by Knight Company during March of the current year.

Mar. 2. Purchased merchandise on account from Sullivan Co., $12,150; terms, n/30.
8. Purchased merchandise on account from Cogan Co., $2,200; terms, 2/10, n/30.
9. Received a credit memorandum from Sullivan Co., $650 for defective merchandise.
16. Issued Check No. 30 to Cogan Co. in payment of the balance due, less 2% discount.
20. Issued Check No. 31 for a cash purchase of merchandise, $1,475.
27. Issued Check No. 32 to Sullivan Co. in payment of the balance due.
28. Purchased the following on account from Parsons & Co.: store supplies, $410, office supplies, $215.

Instructions: Record the above transactions in the purchases journal, cash payments journal, or two-column general journal given below:

PURCHASES JOURNAL — PAGE 15

DATE	ACCOUNT CREDITED	POST. REF.	ACCOUNTS PAYABLE CR.	PURCHASES DR.	STORE SUPPLIES DR.	OFFICE SUPPLIES DR.

CASH PAYMENTS JOURNAL — PAGE 18

DATE	CK. NO.	ACCOUNT DEBITED	POST. REF.	SUNDRY ACCOUNTS DR.	ACCOUNTS PAYABLE DR.	PURCHASES DISCOUNTS CR.	CASH CR.

JOURNAL — PAGE 35

DATE	DESCRIPTION	POST. REF.	DEBIT	CREDIT

PART 6

The "Totals" line and one other line of the purchases journal of Fuller's Hardware Store for the month of June is shown below. Also shown are selected T accounts taken from Fuller's general ledger.

Instructions: (1) Verify the equality of the debits and the credits in the Fuller's Hardware Store purchases journal for June by completing the following schedule:

DEBIT TOTALS		CREDIT TOTALS	
Purchases . . . . $_____		Accounts Payable . . . . $ _____	
Store Supplies . . . . _____			
Office Supplies . . . . _____			
Sundry Accounts . . . . _____			
Total . . . . $_____		Total . . . . $_____	

(2) Post all amounts that require posting to the T accounts provided. Show the appropriate posting references in the purchases journal.

PURCHASES JOURNAL   PAGE 53

DATE	POST. REF.	ACCOUNTS PAYABLE CR.	PURCHASES DR.	STORE SUPPLIES DR.	OFFICE SUPPLIES DR.	SUNDRY ACCOUNTS DR.		
						ACCOUNT	POST. REF.	AMOUNT
30	✓	520 00				Store Equipment		520 00
30		7,290 00	5,250 00	330 00	560 00			1,150 00

GENERAL LEDGER

STORE SUPPLIES   114   OFFICE SUPPLIES   115   STORE EQUIPMENT   121

ACCOUNTS PAYABLE   211   PURCHASES   511

PART 7

During December of the current year, Harrison Co., a retail hardware store, completed the following transactions with customers on account:

Dec. 7. Invoice 310 to Robert Lucas, $185.
     11. Invoice 325 to Jeff Lyle, $260.
     23. Invoice 360 to Pamela Kelley, $470.
     30. Invoice 390 to David Stark, $125.

Instructions: (1) Record the above transactions in the sales journal below.

(2) Post the individual items from the sales journal to the T accounts for customers. Indicate that each item has been posted by placing a check mark (✔) in the Post. Ref. column of the sales journal.

(3) Post the total of the sales journal to the T accounts for Accounts Receivable and Sales. Indicate that the posting is completed by inserting the appropriate account numbers in the journal under the amount posted.

SALES JOURNAL
PAGE 27

DATE	INVOICE NO.	ACCOUNT DEBITED	POST REF.	ACCTS. REC. DR. SALES CR.

GENERAL LEDGER

ACCOUNTS RECEIVABLE   113

SALES   411

ACCOUNTS RECEIVABLE LEDGER

Pamela Kelley

Jeff Lyle

Robert Lucas

David Stark

(4) Determine that the sum of the balances of the individual accounts in the subsidiary accounts receivable ledger agrees with the balance of the accounts receivable controlling account in the general ledger by completing the following summary form.

Pamela Kelley . . . . $ _____

Robert Lucas . . . . _____

Jeff Lyle. . . . . _____

David Stark . . . . _____

Total accounts receivable . . . . $ _____

84

PART 8

The following transactions related to sales and cash receipts were completed by Severhof Co. during February of the current year. The terms of all sales on account are 2/10, n/30, FOB destination.

Feb. 4. Sold merchandise on account to Mears Corp., Invoice No. 883, $9,550.
    5. Sold merchandise on account to Vogler Inc., Invoice No. 884, $4,700.
    9. Issued to Mears Corp. a credit memorandum for merchandise returned. Credit Memo No. 96, $800.
  14. Received cash from Mears Corp. in payment of the $8,750 due on Invoice No. 883, less discount.
  15. Received cash from Vogler Inc. in payment of Invoice No. 884, less discount.
  23. Received cash from office supplies returned to the manufacturer, $245.
  28. Cash sales for February, $37,650.

Instructions: Record the above transactions in the sales journal, cash receipts journal, or two-column general journal given below.

SALES JOURNAL
PAGE 28

DATE	INVOICE NO.	ACCOUNT DEBITED	POST REF.	ACCTS. REC. DR. SALES CR.

CASH RECEIPTS JOURNAL
PAGE 20

DATE	ACCOUNT CREDITED	POST. REF.	SUNDRY ACCOUNTS CR.	SALES CR.	ACCOUNTS REC. CR.	SALES DISCOUNTS DR.	CASH DR.

JOURNAL
PAGE 37

DATE	DESCRIPTION	POST. REF.	DEBIT	CREDIT

Page not used

86

Chapter 8   CASH

STUDY GOALS

After studying this chapter, you should be able to:
1. Explain how a bank account may be used for controlling cash.
2. Prepare a bank reconciliation.
3. Explain how the use of remittance advices, a cash short and over account, and cash change funds may be used to establish internal controls over the handling of cash.
4. Explain how the voucher system may be used for controlling cash payments.
5. Explain how the use of a discounts lost account and a petty cash account may be used for controlling cash payments.
6. Explain how the use of electronic funds transfer may influence the processing of cash transactions.

GLOSSARY OF KEY TERMS

Bank reconciliation. The method of analysis that details the items that are responsible for the difference between the cash balance reported in the bank statement and the balance of the cash account in the ledger.

Check register. A modified form of the cash payments journal used to record all transactions paid by check.

Electronic funds transfer (EFT). A payment system that uses computerized electronic impulses rather than paper (money, checks, etc.) to effect a cash transaction.

Petty cash fund. A special cash fund used to pay relatively small amounts.

Voucher. A document that serves as evidence of authority to pay cash.

Voucher register. The journal in which all vouchers are recorded.

Voucher system. Records, methods, and procedures employed in verifying and recording liabilities and paying and recording cash payments.

CHAPTER OUTLINE

I. Control over Cash.
   A. Because of the ease with which money can be transferred, cash is the asset most likely to be diverted and used improperly by employees. Therefore, cash must be effectively safeguarded by special controls.
   B. One of the major devices for maintaining control over cash is the bank account.
      1. To get the most benefit from a bank account, all cash received must be deposited in the bank and all payments must be made by checks drawn on the bank or from special cash funds.
      2. The forms used by business in connection with a bank account are a signature card, deposit ticket, check, and a record of checks drawn.
      3. The three parties to a check are the drawer, the one who signs the check; the drawee, the bank on which the check is drawn; and the payee, the one to whose order the check is drawn.
      4. A remittance advice is a notification which indicates to a creditor which specific invoice is being paid.
   C. Banks usually mail to each depositor a statement of account once a month which shows the beginning balance, checks and other debits (deductions by the bank), deposits and other credits (additions by the bank), and the balance at the end of the period.
   D. The balance shown on the depositor's records as cash in bank and the ending balance on the bank statement are not likely to be equal on any specific date because of either or both of the following: (1) delay by either party in recording transactions and (2) errors by either party in recording transactions.
   E. To determine the reasons for any difference between the balance according to the bank

statement and the bank balance according to the depositor's records, a bank reconciliation is prepared. The bank reconciliation is divided into two sections: one section begins with the balance according to the bank statement and ends with the adjusted balance; the other section begins with the balance according to the depositor's records and also ends with the adjusted balance. The form and the content of the bank reconciliation are outlined as follows:

Bank balance according to bank statement
Add: Additions by depositor not on bank
statement
    Bank errors

Deduct: Deductions by depositor not on bank
statement
    Bank errors
Adjusted balance
Bank balance according to depositor's records
Add: Additions by bank not recorded by
depositor
    Depositor errors
Deduct: Deductions by bank not recorded by
depositor
    Depositor errors
Adjusted balance

F. The following procedures are used in finding the reconciling items and determining the adjusted balance of cash in bank:
1. Individual deposits listed on the bank statement are compared with unrecorded deposits appearing in the preceding reconciliation and with deposit receipts or other records of deposits. Deposits not recorded by the bank are added to the balance according to the bank statement.
2. Paid checks are compared with outstanding checks appearing on the preceding reconciliation and with checks listed in the cash payments journal. Checks issued that have not been paid by the bank are outstanding and are deducted from the balance according to the bank statement.
3. Bank credit memorandums are traced to the cash receipts journal. Credit memorandums not recorded in the cash receipts journal are added to the balance according to the depositor's records.
4. Bank debit memorandums are traced to the cash payments journal. Debit memorandums not recorded in the cash payments journal are deducted from the balance according to the depositor's records.
5. Errors discovered during the process of making the foregoing comparisons are listed separately on the reconciliation. For example, if the amount for which a check was written had been recorded erroneously by the depositor, the amount of the error

should be added to or deducted from the balance according to the depositor's records. Similarly, errors by the bank should be added to or deducted from the balance according to the bank statement.
G. Bank memorandums not recorded by the depositor and depositor's errors shown by the bank reconciliation require that entries be made in the accounts.
1. The data needed for these adjustments are provided by the section of the bank reconciliation that begins with the balance per depositor's records.
2. After the adjusting entries are posted, the cash in bank account will have a balance which agrees with the adjusted balance shown on the bank reconciliation.
H. The bank reconciliation is an important part of the internal controls because it is a means of comparing recorded cash, as shown by the accounting records, with the amount of cash recorded by the bank.
1. Greater internal controls are achieved when the bank reconciliation is prepared by an employee who does not take part in or record cash transactions with the bank.
2. Without a proper separation of duties, cash is more likely to be embezzled.
II. Internal Control of Cash Receipts.
A. The employees who open incoming mail should compare the amount of cash received with the amount shown on the accompanying remittance advice to make sure the two amounts agree. The cash should then be forwarded to the cashier's department and the remittance advices should be delivered to the accounting department for proper recording.
B. When the amount of cash actually received during the day does not agree with the record of cash receipts, the difference should be debited or credited to a cash short and over account.
1. A debit balance in the cash short and over account at the end of the fiscal period is listed as an expense on the income statement. A credit balance is listed as a revenue.
2. If the balance of the cash short and over account becomes larger than may be accounted for by minor errors, management should take corrective measures.
C. Businesses that receive cash directly from customers and that must make change utilize a cash on hand account. At the end of each business day, the total amount of cash received during the day is deposited and the original amount of the cash fund is retained.
III. Internal Control of Cash Payments.
A. It is common practice for business enterprises to require that every payment of cash be evi-

denced by a check through use of a voucher system.

B. A voucher system is made up of records, methods, and procedures used in proving and recording liabilities and making and recording cash payments. A voucher system normally has the following components:

1. A voucher is a special form on which is recorded relevant data about a liability and the details of its payment. Vouchers are customarily prepared by the accounting department on the basis of an invoice or a memorandum that serves as proof of an expenditure.

2. In a voucher system, the voucher register replaces the purchases journal and is the record in which all vouchers are entered in numerical order. Each voucher represents a credit to accounts payable (sometimes entitled vouchers payable) and a debit to the account or accounts to be charged for the expenditure. When a voucher is paid, the date of payment and the number of the check are inserted in the proper columns in the voucher register.

3. After a voucher has been recorded in the voucher register, it is filed in an unpaid voucher file where it remains until it is paid. The amount due on each voucher represents the credit balance of an account payable, and the voucher itself is like an individual account in a subsidiary accounts payable ledger. A voucher is filed in the unpaid voucher file according to the earliest date that consideration should be given to its payment. When a voucher is paid, it is removed from the unpaid voucher file and a check is issued for payment. Paid vouchers and the supporting documents should be canceled to prevent accidental or intentional reuse.

4. The payment of a voucher is recorded in a check register. The check register is a modified form of the cash payments journal and is so called because it is a complete record of all checks.

5. After payment, vouchers are usually filed in numerical order in a paid voucher file.

6. The voucher system not only provides effective accounting controls but it also aids management in making the best use of cash resources and in planning cash disbursements.

C. Discounts on the purchase of merchandise will be accounted for as either deductions from purchases or as other income.

1. A major disadvantage of recording purchases at the invoice price and recognizing purchases discounts at the time of payment as a deduction for purchases is that this method does not measure the cost of failing to take purchases discounts.

2. By recording purchases at the net amount (assuming that all discounts would be taken) and using a discounts lost account, better control can be maintained over the taking of cash discounts.

3. When the net method of recording purchases is used, all vouchers are prepared and recorded at the net amount. Any discount lost is noted on the related voucher and recorded in a special column in the check register when the voucher is paid.

D. A petty cash fund may be used by businesses for which there is a frequent need for the payment of relatively small amounts, such as for postage due, etc.

1. In establishing a petty cash fund, the account Petty Cash is debited. If a voucher system is used, Accounts Payable (or Vouchers Payable) is credited. When the check is drawn to pay the voucher, Accounts Payable (Vouchers Payable) is debited and Cash in Bank is credited.

2. The petty cash fund is replenished by a general journal entry debiting the various expense and asset accounts and crediting Accounts Payable (Vouchers Payable). The check in payment of the voucher is recorded in the usual manner.

3. Because disbursements are not recorded in the accounts until the fund is replenished, petty cash funds and other special funds that operate in a like manner should always be replenished at the end of an accounting period.

E. Cash funds may also be established to meet other special needs of a business. These funds are accounted for in a similar fashion as a petty cash fund.

IV. Cash Transactions and Electronic Funds Transfer.

A. Electronic funds transfer is a payment system which uses computerized electronic impulses rather than paper (money, checks, etc.) to effect cash transactions.

B. EFT is beginning to play an important role in retail sales through such systems as the point-of-sale (POS) system.

PART 1

Instructions: A list of terms and related statements appear below. From the list of terms, select the one that relates to each statement and print its identifying letter in the space provided.

A. Bank reconciliation   **E.** Electronic funds transfer   **H.** Unpaid voucher file
B. Check register   **F.** Petty cash   **I.** Voucher
C. Compensating balance   **G.** Remittance advice   **J.** Voucher register
D. Drawer

_____ **1.** The party signing a check.

_____ **2.** A required minimum cash balance maintained in a bank account, generally imposed by the bank as part of a loan agreement.

_____ **3.** A notification which accompanies checks issued to a creditor that indicates the specific invoice that is being paid.

_____ **4.** An accounting record in which the bank balance according to the bank statement is reconciled with the bank balance according to the depositor's records.

_____ **5.** A special form on which is recorded relevant data about a liability and the details of its payment.

_____ **6.** After a voucher has been recorded in the voucher register, it is filed in a(n) (?)

_____ **7.** After approval by the designated official, each voucher is recorded in the (?)

_____ **8.** A modified form of the cash payments journal used for recording cash payments when a voucher system is in use.

_____ **9.** A special cash fund set aside for the payment of relatively small amounts for which payment by check is not efficient.

_____ **10.** A payment system using computerized electronic impulses rather than paper to effect a cash transaction.

Name _____

PART 2

Instructions: Indicate whether each of the following statements is true or false by placing a check mark in the appropriate column.

		True	False
1.	There are four parties to a check	____	____
2.	The payee is the one to whose order the check is drawn.	____	____
3.	In a bank reconciliation, checks issued that have not been paid by the bank are added to the balance according to the bank statement	____	____
4.	Bank memorandums not recorded by the depositor require entries in the depositor's accounts . . .	____	____
5.	For a greater degree of internal control, the bank reconciliation should be prepared by an employee who does not engage in or record cash transactions with the bank	____	____
6.	If there is a debit balance in the cash short and over account at the end of the fiscal period, this represents income to be included in "Miscellaneous general income" in the income statement. . .	____	____
7.	It is common practice for business enterprises to require that every payment of cash be evidenced by a check signed by the owner.	____	____
8.	After vouchers are paid, it is customary to file them in numerical sequence in the paid voucher file.	____	____
9.	It is a widely accepted view that purchases discounts should be reported as deductions from purchases.	____	____
10.	Petty Cash should be debited when the petty cash fund is replenished.	____	____

PART 3

Instructions: Complete each of the following statements by circling the letter of the best answer.

1. The bank on which a check is drawn is known as the
   a. drawer
   b. drawee
   c. payee
   d. creditor

2. In a bank reconciliation, deposits not recorded by the bank are
   a. added to the balance according to the bank statement
   b. deducted from the balance according to the bank statement
   c. added to the balance according to the depositor's records
   d. deducted from the balance according to the depositor's records

3. For good internal control over cash receipts, remittance advices should be separated from cash received by mail and should be sent directly to the
   a. treasurer
   b. cashier's department
   c. accounting department
   d. voucher clerk

4. An important characteristic of the voucher system is the requirement that
   a. vouchers be prepared by the treasurer
   b. vouchers be paid immediately after they are prepared
   c. the face of the voucher show the account distribution
   d. a voucher be prepared for each expenditure

5. In a voucher system, the entry to record the replenishment of the petty cash fund includes a debit to various expense and asset accounts and a credit to
   a. Cash in Bank
   b. Petty Cash
   c. Accounts Payable
   d. various liability accounts

Name _____

PART 4

On June 30 of the current year, Bradshaw Co.'s checkbook showed a balance of $8,960 and the bank statement showed a balance of $9,510. A comparison of the bank statement and Bradshaw's records as of June 30 revealed the following:

(a) A deposit of $1,850, mailed to the bank by Bradshaw on June 29, was not included in the bank statement of June 30.

(b) The following checks were outstanding:

      Check No. 255 for $290
      Check No. 280 for $135
      Check No. 295 for $710

(c) Check No. 289 in payment of a voucher had been written for $240 and had been recorded at that amount by the bank. However, Bradshaw had recorded it in the check register as $420.

(d) A check for $820 received from a customer was deposited in the bank. The bank recorded it at the correct amount, but Bradshaw recorded it at $280.

(e) Included with the bank statement was a credit memorandum for $570, representing the proceeds of a $500 note receivable left at the bank for collection. This had not been recorded on Bradshaw's books.

(f) Included with the bank statement was a debit memorandum for $25 for service charges which had not been recorded on Bradshaw's books.

Instructions: (1) Complete the following bank reconciliation:

Bradshaw Co.
Bank Reconciliation
June 30, 19—

Balance according to bank statement .... $
Add:

Deduct:

Adjusted balance .... $_____

Balance according to depositor's records .... $
Add:

Deduct:

Adjusted balance .... $_____

(2) In the following general journal, prepare the entry or entries that Bradshaw Co. should make as a result of the bank reconciliation.

Shields Gift Shop Co. uses a voucher system. On June 1 of the current year, Shields issued Voucher No. 225 to record the purchase of $950 of novelty items from Nixon Co., terms 2/10, n/30. Also on June 1, Shields issued Voucher No. 226 to record the purchase of $800 of leather goods from Strange Inc., terms 2/10, n/30, and Voucher No. 227 to record the purchase of $1,300 of stuffed animals from Ranger Corp., terms 1/10, n/30.

Shields issued the following checks: June 5, Check No. 710 in payment of Voucher No. 225; June 8, Check No. 711 in payment of Voucher No. 227; June 15, Check No. 712 in payment of Voucher No. 226.

Instructions: (1) Record the vouchers in the partial voucher register below.

VOUCHER REGISTER

DATE	VOU. NO.	PAYEE	DATE PAID	CK. NO.	ACCOUNTS PAYABLE CR.	PURCHASES DR.

(2) Record the checks in the check register below. (Bank Deposits and Balance columns are omitted.) Also make the appropriate notations in the voucher register above.

CHECK REGISTER   PAGE

DATE	CK. NO.	PAYEE	VOU. NO.	ACCOUNTS PAYABLE DR.	PURCHASES DISCOUNTS CR.	CASH CR.

PART 6

Instructions: Record the following transactions in the general journal provided below, assuming that invoices for commodities purchased are recorded at their net price after deducting the allowable discount.

June   5 Voucher No. 560 is prepared for merchandise purchased from Bonds Co., $3,700, terms 2/10, n/60.
     9 Voucher No. 561 is prepared for merchandise purchased from Meek Co., $13,500, terms 1/10, n/30.
   19 Check No. 210 is issued, payable to Meek Co., in payment of Voucher No. 561.
July   7 Check No. 217 is issued, payable to Bonds Co., in payment of Voucher No. 560.

JOURNAL   PAGE

DATE		DESCRIPTION	POST. REF.	DEBIT	CREDIT

PART 7

Instructions: In the general journal provided below, prepare the entries to record the following transactions:

(1) Voucher No. 357 is prepared to establish a petty cash fund of $400.

(2) Check No. 805 is issued in payment of Voucher No. 357.

(3) The amount of cash in the petty cash fund is now $162.15. Voucher No. 461 is prepared to replenish the fund, based on the following summary of petty cash receipts:

Office supplies, $72.12
Miscellaneous selling expense, $115.38
Miscellaneous general expense, $52.84

(4) Check No. 844 is issued by the disbursing officer in payment of Voucher No. 461. The check is cashed and the money is placed in the fund.

JOURNAL   PAGE

DATE	DESCRIPTION	POST. REF.	DEBIT	CREDIT

RECEIVABLES AND TEMPORARY INVESTMENTS

STUDY GOALS

After studying this chapter, you should be able to:
1. List the common classifications of receivables.
2. List the basic principles of internal control over receivables.
3. Prepare journal entries for recording notes receivable, including interest and the proceeds from discounting notes.
4. Prepare journal entries for the allowance method of accounting for uncollectible receivables, including the write-off of uncollectible receivables and the esti-

mation of receivables based upon sales and an analysis of the receivables.
5. Prepare journal entries for the direct write-off method of accounting for uncollectible receivables.
6. Summarize the accounting for temporary investments, including the lower of cost or market rule.
7. Prepare the current asset section of a balance sheet, including the presentation of temporary investments and receivables.

GLOSSARY OF KEY TERMS

Aging the receivables. The process of analyzing the accounts receivable and classifying them according to various age groupings, with the due date being the base point for determining age.

Allowance method. The method of accounting for uncollectible receivables, by which advance provision for the uncollectibles is made.

Carrying amount. The amount at which a temporary or a long-term investment or a long-term liability is reported on the balance sheet; also called basis or book value.

Contingent liability. A potential obligation that will materialize only if certain events occur in the future.

Direct write-off method. A method of accounting for uncollectible receivables, whereby an expense is recognized only when specific accounts are judged to be uncollectible.

Discount. The interest deducted from the maturity value of a note.

Dishonored note receivable. A note which the maker fails to pay on the due date.

Marketable security. An investment in a security that can be readily sold when cash is needed.

Maturity value. The amount due at the maturity or due date of a note.

Note receivable. A written promise to pay, representing an amount owed by a business.

Proceeds. The net amount available from discounting a note.

Promissory note. A written promise to pay a sum in money on demand or at a definite time.

Temporary investment. An investment in securities that can be readily sold when cash is needed.

CHAPTER OUTLINE

I. Classification of Receivables.
  A. The term receivables includes all money claims against people, organizations, or other debtors.
    1. A promissory note is a written promise to pay a sum of money on demand or at a definite time. The one to whose order the note is payable is called the payee, and the

one making the promise is called the maker. The enterprise owning a note refers to it as a note receivable and records it as an asset at its face value.
    2. A note that provides for payment of interest is called an interest-bearing note. If a note makes no provision for interest, it is said to be non-interest-bearing.

3. The amount that is due at the maturity or due date of a note is called the maturity value.
4. Accounts and notes receivable originating from sales transactions are called trade receivables.
5. Other receivables include interest receivable, loans to officers or employees, and loans to affiliated companies.

B. All receivables that are expected to be realized in cash within a year are presented as current assets on the balance sheet. Those not currently collectible, such as long-term loans, are shown as investments.

II. Control Over Receivables.
A. The broad principles of internal control should be used to establish procedures to safeguard receivables. These controls include the following:
1. Separation of the business operations and the accounting for receivables.
2. The maintenance of subsidiary records and ledgers for accounts and notes receivable.
3. Proper approval of all credit sales by a responsible official or the credit department.
4. Proper approval of all sales returns and allowances and sales discounts.
5. Effective collection procedures to minimize losses from uncollectible accounts.

B. The proper use of the above control procedures decreases the risk of loss from the granting of credit.

III. Determining Interest.
A. The basic formula for computing interest is as follows:

Principal × Rate × Time = Interest

B. Interest rates are usually stated in terms of a period of a year, regardless of the actual period of time involved.
C. For purposes of computing interest, the commercial practice of using 1/12 of a year for a month and a 360-day year will be utilized.

IV. Determining Due Date.
A. The term of time between the issuance date and the maturity date of a short-term note may be stated either in days or months.
B. When the term of a note is stated in days, the due date is a specified number of days after its issuance.
C. When the term of a note is stated as a certain number of months after the issuance date, the due date is determined by counting the number of months from the issuance date. For example, a three-month note dated July 31 would be due on October 31.

V. Notes Receivable and Interest Income.
A. When a note is received from a customer to apply on account, notes receivable is debited and accounts receivable is credited for the face amount of the note.
B. At the end of the fiscal year, an adjusting entry is necessary to record the accrued interest on any outstanding notes receivable.
C. To facilitate the recording of the receipt of the maturity amount of the note and interest on the due date, a reversing entry is made as of the first day of the accounting period for any accrued interest recorded from the prior period.
D. At the time a note matures and payment is received, Cash is debited, Notes Receivable is credited for the face amount of the note, and Interest Income is credited for the amount of interest due.
E. Instead of retaining a note until maturity, notes receivable may be transferred to a bank by endorsement, a process known as discounting notes receivable.
1. The interest (discount) charged by the bank is computed on the maturity value of the note for the period of time the bank must hold the note, namely the time that will pass between the date of the transfer and the due date of the note.
2. The amount of the proceeds paid to the endorser is the excess of the maturity value over the discount.
3. The entry to record the discounting of notes receivable is to debit Cash for the proceeds, credit Notes Receivable for the face value of the note, and either debit Interest Expense or credit Interest Income for the amount to balance the entry.
4. If a maker of the note defaults on a note that has been discounted at a bank, a contingent liability may arise to the initial holder of the note for the face amount of the note plus accrued interest and any protest fee. Any significant contingent liabilities should be disclosed on the balance sheet or in an accompanying note.

F. If the maker of the note fails to pay the debt on the due date, the note is said to be dishonored. The entry for a dishonored note is to debit Accounts Receivable for the maturity amount of the note, credit Notes Receivable for the face value of the note, and credit Interest Income for the amount of interest due on the note at maturity. When a discounted note receivable is dishonored, the holder usually notifies the endorser and asks for payment. If request for payment and notification of dishonor are timely, the endorser is legally obligated to pay the amount due on the note.
1. The holder of a dishonored note may charge a fee, known as a protest fee, to the endorser of the note.
2. Any protest fee which is paid by the endorser is debited to the account receivable of the original maker of the note.

VI. Uncollectible Receivables.
   A. When merchandise or services are sold on credit, a part of the claims against customers usually proves to be uncollectible.
   B. The operating expense incurred because of the failure to collect receivables is called uncollectible accounts expense, doubtful accounts expense, or bad debts.
   C. The two methods of accounting for receivables believed to be uncollectible are the allowance method and the direct write-off method.
VII. Allowance Method of Accounting for Uncollectibles.
   A. Under the allowance method of accounting for uncollectibles, advance provision for uncollectibility is made by an adjusting entry at the end of the fiscal period.
      1. The adjusting entry to record the allowance for uncollectibles is to debit Uncollectible Accounts Expense and credit Allowance for Doubtful Accounts. The account Allowance for Doubtful Accounts is a contra asset account offsetting accounts receivable.
      2. The balance of the accounts receivable account less the contra account, Allowance for Doubtful Accounts, determines the expected realizable value of the receivables as of the end of the fiscal period.
      3. Uncollectible accounts expense is recorded on the income statement as a general expense and is closed to Income Summary.
   B. When an account is believed to be uncollectible, it is written off against the allowance account by debiting Allowance for Doubtful Accounts and crediting the customer's account receivable.
   C. An account receivable that has been written off against the allowance account may later be collected.
      1. The account should be reinstated by an entry that is the exact reverse of the write-off entry — a debit to the customer's account receivable and a credit to Allowance for Doubtful Accounts.
      2. The cash received in payment would be recorded in the usual manner as a debit to Cash and a credit to Accounts Receivable.
   D. The estimate of uncollectibles at the end of the fiscal period is based on past experience and forecasts of future business activity. Two methods of estimating uncollectibles are as follows:
      1. The amount of uncollectibles may be estimated based upon the percentage of sales.
         a. Based upon past experience or industry averages, the percentage of sales which will prove to be uncollectible is esti-mated.
         b. The estimated percentage of uncollectible sales is then multiplied by the sales for the period and Uncollectible Accounts Expense is debited and Allowance for Doubtful Accounts is credited for this amount.
         c. The estimated perentage should ideally be based upon credit sales, but total sales may be used if the portion of credit sales to total sales is relatively stable.
      2. Uncollectibles may be estimated by analyzing the individual account receivable accounts in terms of length of time past due.
         a. An aging of accounts receivable is prepared which lists accounts by due date.
         b. Percentages are applied to each category of past due accounts to estimate the balance of the allowance for doubtful accounts as of the end of the accounting period.
         c. The amount of the adjusting entry at the end of the fiscal period for uncollectible accounts expense is determined by that amount necessary to bring the allowance account to its estimated balance as of the end of the period.
   E. Estimates of uncollectible accounts expense based on analysis of the receivables are less common than estimates based on sales.
VIII. Direct Write-Off Method of Accounting for Uncollectibles.
   A. Under the direct write-off method of accounting for uncollectibles, no entry is made for uncollectibility until an account is determined to be worthless. At that time, an entry is made debiting Uncollectible Accounts Expense and crediting the individual customer's account receivable.
   B. If the account that has been written off is later collected, the account should be reinstated by reversing the earlier entry to write off the account.
   C. The receipt of cash and payment of a reinstated account is recorded in the usual manner.
IX. Temporary Investments.
   A. Most businesses invest idle or excess cash in temporary investments or marketable securities. These securities can be quickly sold when cash is needed.
   B. Temporary investments and securities include stocks and bonds. Stocks are equity securities issued by corporations and bonds are debt securities issued by corporations and various government agencies.
   C. A temporary investment in a portfolio of

debt securities is carried at cost.

D. A temporary investment in a portfolio of equity securities is carried at the lower of its total cost or market value determined at the date of the balance sheet.

1. Note that the carrying amount is based upon the total cost and total market value of the portfolio, rather than the lower of cost or market price of each individual equity security.

2. If the total market value of the equity securities is less than cost, an unrealized loss is recorded and reported on the income statement as a separate item.

3. If the market value of the portfolio later rises, the unrealized loss is reversed and included in the income, but only to the extent that it does not exceed the original cost. In such cases, the increase is reported separately in the Other Income section of the income statement.

X. Temporary Investments and Receivables in the Balance Sheet.

A. Temporary investments and all receivables that are expected to be realized in cash within a year are presented in the current assets section of the balance sheet.

B. It is customary to list the assets in the order of their liquidity, that is, in the order in which they can be converted to cash in normal operations.

Name _____

PART 1

Instructions: A list of terms and related statements appear below. From the list of terms, select the one that relates to each statement and print its identifying letter in the space provided.

A. Aging the receivables
B. Allowance method
C. Contingent liabilities
D. Direct write-off method

E. Discount
F. Dishonored
G. Expected realizable value
H. Proceeds

I. Promissory note
J. Temporary investments

_____ **1.** A written promise to pay a sum of money on demand or at a definite time.

_____ **2.** The interest charged by a bank for discounting a note receivable.

_____ **3.** The amount received from selling a note receivable prior to its maturity.

_____ **4.** Potential obligations that will become actual liabilities only if certain events occur in the future.

_____ **5.** If the maker of a note fails to pay the debt on the due date, the note is said to be (?)

_____ **6.** A method of accounting for receivables which provides in advance for uncollectible receivables through the use of an allowance for doubtful accounts.

_____ **7.** A method of accounting for uncollectible receivables in which no expense is recognized until individual accounts are determined to be worthless.

_____ **8.** The balance of the accounts receivable following the deduction of the allowance for doubtful accounts.

_____ **9.** The process of analyzing the receivable accounts in terms of the length of time past due.

_____ **10.** Securities that may be quickly sold when cash is needed.

PART 2

Instructions: Indicate whether each of the following statements is true or false by placing a check mark in the appropriate column.

	True	False
1. The term "notes" includes all money claims against people, organizations, or other debtors	_____	_____
2. Accounts and notes receivable originating from sales transactions are sometimes called trade receivables..	_____	_____
3. For good internal control, an employee who handles the accounting for notes and accounts receivable should not be involved with credit approvals or collections of receivables	_____	_____
4. When a note is received from a customer on account, it is recorded by debiting Notes Receivable and crediting Cash	_____	_____
5. When the holder transfers a note to a bank by endorsement, the discount (interest) charged is computed on the face value of the note for the period of time the bank must hold the note.......	_____	_____
6. When the proceeds from discounting a note receivable are less than the face value, the difference is recorded as interest expense	_____	_____
7. The endorser of a note that has been discounted has a contingent liability that is in effect until the due date	_____	_____
8. The method of accounting which provides in advance for receivables deemed uncollectible is called the reserve or net realizable value method..	_____	_____
9. The process of analyzing the receivable accounts in order to estimate the uncollectibles is sometimes called aging the receivables	_____	_____
10. The carrying amount of a temporary investment in equity securities is the lower of its total cost or market value..	_____	_____

PART 3

Instructions: Complete each of the following statements by circling the letter of the best answer.

1. On a promissory note, the one making the promise to pay is called the
   a. payee
   b. creditor
   c. maker
   d. noter

2. The amount that is due on a note at the maturity or due date is called the
   a. terminal value
   b. face value
   c. book value
   d. maturity value

3. When a note is discounted, the excess of the maturity value over the discount is called the
   a. gain
   b. proceeds
   c. interest
   d. present value

4. When the allowance method is used in accounting for uncollectible accounts, any uncollectible account is written off against the
   a. allowance account
   b. sales account
   c. accounts receivable account
   d. uncollectible accounts expense account

5. Assume that the allowance account has a credit balance at year end of $270 before adjustment. If the estimate of uncollectible accounts based on aging the receivables is $3,010, the amount of the adjusting entry for uncollectible accounts would be
   a. $270
   b. $2,740
   c. $3,010
   d. $3,280

PART 4

Instructions: Using the basic formula for interest and assuming a 360-day year, compute the interest on the following notes.

1. $8,000 at 12% for 30 days . . . . $ _____

2. $3,000 at 6% for 60 days . . . . $ _____

3. $2,000 at 14% for 90 days . . . . $ _____

Instructions: Using the 60-day, 6% method, complete the following interest calculations. (Problems 4 and 5 are the same as 1 and 2, so that the two methods of computing interest may be compared.)

4. The interest on $8,000 at 12% for 30 days is . . . . $ _____

5. The interest on $3,000 at 6% for 60 days is . . . . $ _____

6. The interest on $12,000 for 60 days at 10% is . . . . $ _____

7. The interest on $4,000 for 120 days at 15% is . . . . $ _____

PART 5

Instructions: Based on the information given, fill in the blanks below.

(1) A 10%, 90-day note receivable for $6,000 was discounted at 11%, 20 days after date.

Face value .... _____

Interest on face value .... _____

Maturity value.. _____

Discount on maturity value .... _____

Proceeds .... _____

(2) A 12%, 120-day note receivable for $7,000 was discounted at 14%, 15 days after date.

Face value .... _____

Interest on face value .... _____

Maturity value.. _____

Discount on maturity value .... _____

Proceeds .... _____

PART 6

Instructions: Prepare the general journal entries to record the following transactions. (Omit explanations.)

(1) Boone Co. received a 90-day, 13% note for $4,500 from a customer, Bevo Davis, in settlement of Davis' account.

(2) Twenty days after the date of the note in (1), Boone discounted Davis' note at the bank at 11%.

(3) Davis failed to pay the note in (1) and (2) at maturity. Boone paid the bank.

(4) Twenty days after the maturity of the note in (1), (2), and (3), Davis paid Boone in full, including interest at 12% for this 20-day period.

(5) Boone Co. received a 90-day, 10% note for $2,000 from a customer, Mark Walker, in settlement of Walker's account.

(6) The note in (5) was dishonored at maturity.

PART 7

Instructions: Prepare the appropriate general journal entries for each of the following situations.

(1) Net sales for the year are $520,000, uncollectible accounts expense is estimated at 2% of net sales, and the allowance account has a $375 credit balance before adjustment. Prepare the adjusting entry at year end for the uncollectibles.

(2) Based on an analysis of accounts in the customers ledger, estimated uncollectible accounts total $2,750, and the allowance account has a $150 credit balance before adjustment. Prepare the adjusting entry at year end for the uncollectibles.

(3) A $3,300 account receivable from Richmond Co. is written off as uncollectible. The allowance method is used.

(4) A $1,900 account receivable from Smith Co., which was written off three months earlier, is collected in full. The allowance method is used.

PART 8

Young Co. uses the direct write-off method of accounting for uncollectibles. On August 31, 1987, Young deemed that an amount of $325 due from Rich Lewis was uncollectible and wrote it off. On October 10, 1987, Lewis paid the $325.

Instructions:

(1) Prepare the entry to write off the account on August 31.

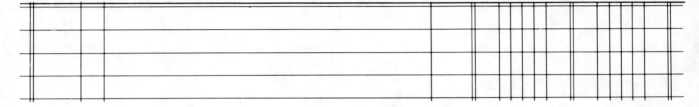

(2) Prepare the entries to reinstate the account on October 10 and to record the cash received.

PART 9

Ayle Co. had a temporary investment in a portfolio of equity securities as of December 31, 1987, as follows:

	Cost	Market
Security A	$15,000	$10,000
Security B	$18,000	$19,000
Security C	$16,000	$20,000
Security D	$18,000	$16,000

Instructions: Compute the proper carrying amount of these securities on Ayle's December 31, 1987

balance sheet ....$ _____

Page not used

Chapter 10

INVENTORIES

STUDY GOALS

After studying this chapter, you should be able to:

1. Explain how the misstatements of inventory affect the financial statements for the current period and the following period.
2. List and describe the two principal inventory systems.
3. Explain how the actual quantity in inventory is determined at year end.
4. List the most common methods of determining cost of inventory and explain how the choice of inventory costing methods affects the operating results.
5. Value inventory at the lower of cost or market.
6. Prepare journal entries for a perpetual inventory system.
7. Prepare the proper presentation of inventory for the financial statements.
8. Estimate inventory using the retail method and the gross profit method.

GLOSSARY OF KEY TERMS

Average cost method. The method of inventory costing that is based on the assumption that costs should be charged against revenue in accordance with the weighted average unit costs of the commodities sold.

First-in, first-out (fifo) method. A method of inventory costing based on the assumption that the costs of merchandise sold should be charged against revenue in the order in which the costs were incurred.

Gross profit method. A means of estimating inventory on hand without the need for a physical count.

Last-in, first-out (lifo) method. A method of inventory costing based on the assumption that the most recent merchandise costs incurred should be charged against revenue.

Lower of cost or market. A method of costing inventory or valuing temporary investments that carries those assets at the lower of their cost or current market prices.

Merchandise inventory. Merchandise on hand and available for sale.

Net realizable value. The amount at which merchandise that can be sold only at prices below cost should be valued, determined as the estimated selling price less any direct cost of disposition.

Periodic inventory system. A system of inventory accounting in which only the revenue from sales is recorded each time a sale is made; the cost of merchandise on hand at the end of a period is determined by a detailed listing (physical inventory) of the merchandise on hand.

Perpetual inventory system. A system of inventory accounting that employs records that continually disclose the amount of the inventory on hand.

Retail inventory method. A method of inventory costing based on the relationship of the cost and retail price of merchandise.

CHAPTER OUTLINE

I. Importance of Inventories.
   A. Inventory has an important effect on the current period's financial statements.
      1. Inventory determination plays an important role in matching expired costs with revenues of the period.
      2. The cost of merchandise at the end of the period will appear on the balance sheet as a current asset.
      3. The inventories at the beginning and the end of the period will affect the cost of merchandise sold, which is deducted from net sales to yield gross profit.
      4. An overstatement in the determination of inventory at the end of the accounting period will cause an overstatement of

gross profit and net income on the income statement and an overstatement of assets and owner's equity on the balance sheet.

    5. An understatement of inventory at the end of the accounting period will cause an understatement of gross profit and net income on the income statement, and an understatement of assets and owner's equity on the balance sheet.

B. Since the inventory at the end of one period becomes the beginning inventory for the following period, misstatements of inventory will affect the following period's financial statements.

    1. If the inventory is incorrectly stated at the end of the period, the net income of that period will be misstated and so will the net income for the following period.

    2. The amount of the two misstatements of net income will be equal and in opposite directions. Therefore, the effect on net income of an incorrectly stated inventory, if not corrected, is limited to the period of the error and the following period. At the end of the period subsequent to the period of an uncorrected error, the balance sheet will be properly stated. This is because the two misstatements of net income will cancel each other.

C. The effect of misstatements of beginning inventory have the opposite effect on the income statement and balance sheet as the same misstatements of ending inventory would have on the income statement and balance sheet.

II. Inventory Systems.

A. The two principal systems of inventory accounting are the periodic and perpetual inventory systems.

    1. When the periodic inventory system is used, only the revenue from sales is recorded each time a sale is made. No entry is made at the time of the sale to record the cost of the merchandise that has been sold. A physical inventory must be taken in order to determine the cost of the inventory at the end of the accounting period and the associated cost of merchandise sold for the period.

    2. The perpetual inventory system uses accounting records that continuously disclose the amount of inventory. Purchases of inventory items are recorded at the time of purchase as debits to the proper inventory accounts, and sales of inventory are recorded as credits at the time of sale. The balances of the accounts are called book inventories of the items on hand.

B. Although much of the discussion in this chapter applies to both systems, the use of the periodic inventory system will be normally assumed.

III. Determining Actual Quantities in the Inventory.

A. The actual quantities of inventory at the end of an accounting period are determined by the process of "taking" an inventory.

B. All the merchandise owned by the business on the inventory date, and only such merchandise, should be included in the inventory.

C. It may be necessary to examine purchase and sales invoices of the last few days of the accounting period and the first few days of the following period to determine who has legal title to merchandise in transit on the inventory date.

    1. When goods are purchased or sold FOB shipping point, title usually passes to the buyer when the goods are shipped. Therefore, these items should be included in inventory by the purchaser on the shipping date.

    2. When goods are purchased or sold FOB destination, title usually does not pass to the buyer until the goods are delivered. Therefore, goods shipped under these terms should be included in inventory by the purchaser only when the goods have been received.

D. Special care should be taken for accounting for merchandise that has been shipped on a consignment basis to a retailer (the consignee). Even though the manufacturer does not have physical possession, consigned merchandise should be included in the manufacturer's (the consignor's) inventory.

IV. Determining the Cost of Inventory.

A. The cost of merchandise inventory is made up of the purchase price and all expenditures incurred in acquiring such merchandise, including such costs as transportation, customs duties, and insurance.

B. If purchases discounts are treated as a deduction from purchases on the income statement, they should also be deducted from the purchase price of the items in the inventory.

V. Inventory Costing Methods Under a Periodic System.

A. One of the most significant problems in determining inventory cost comes about when identical units of a certain commodity have been acquired at different unit cost prices during the period. In such cases, it is necessary to determine the unit prices of the items still on hand.

B. Under specific identification procedures, it may be possible to identify units with specific expenditures if both the variety of merchandise carried in stock and the volume of sales are relatively small. Ordinarily, however, specific identification procedures are not used.

C. If specific identification procedures are not used, an arbitrary assumption as to the flow of costs of merchandise through the enterprise must be made. The three most common assumptions of determining the cost of merchandise sold are as follows:

1. Cost flow is in the order in which the expenditures were made — first-in, first-out.

2. Cost flow is in the reverse order in which the expenditures were made — last-in, first-out.

3. Cost flow is an average of the expenditures.

D. The first-in, first-out (fifo) method of costing inventory is based on the assumption that costs should be charged against revenue in the order in which they are incurred.

1. The inventory remaining at the end of the period is assumed to be made up of the most recent costs.

2. The fifo method is generally in harmony with the physical movement of merchandise in an enterprise. To this extent, the fifo method approximates the results that would be obtained by the specific identification of costs.

E. The last-in, first-out (lifo) method is based on the assumption that the most recent costs incurred should be charged against revenue.

1. The inventory remaining at the end of the period is assumed to be composed of the earliest costs.

2. Even though it does not represent the physical flow of the goods, the lifo method is widely used in business today.

F. The average cost method, sometimes called the weighted average method, is based on the assumption that costs should be charged against revenue according to the weighted average unit costs of the goods sold.

1. The same weighted average unit costs are used in determining the cost of the merchandise remaining in the inventory and the cost of merchandise sold.

2. For businesses in which various purchases of identical units of a commodity are mixed together, the average method has some relationship to the physical flow of goods.

G. A comparison of the inventory costing methods reveals that each method is based on a different assumption as to the flow of costs.

1. If the cost of units and prices at which they are sold remains stable, all three methods yield the same results.

2. Prices do change, however, and as a consequence the three methods will yield different amounts for ending inventory and the cost of merchandise sold for the period.

3. In periods of rising prices, the fifo method yields the lowest cost of merchandise sold, the highest net income, and the highest amount for ending inventory.

4. In periods of rising prices, the lifo method yields the highest cost of merchandise sold, the lowest net income, and the lowest ending inventory.

5. In periods of changing prices, the average cost method yields results that are in between those of fifo and lifo.

H. During periods of rising prices, most companies prefer to use the last-in, first-out method to reduce the amount of income taxes.

I. It is not unusual for businesses to apply different inventory costing methods to different types of inventory. The method used by a company for inventory costing purposes should be properly disclosed in the financial statements. In addition, any changes in methods should also be disclosed.

VI. Valuation of Inventory at Other than Cost.

A. Although cost is the primary basis for the valuation of inventories, under certain circumstances inventory may be valued at other than cost.

B. If the market price of an inventory item is lower than its cost, the lower of cost or market method may be used.

1. Market means the cost to replace the merchandise on the inventory date, based on quantities purchased from the usual source of supply.

2. The use of the lower of cost or market method provides two advantages: the gross profit is reduced for the period in which the decline occurred, and an approximately normal gross profit is realized during the period in which the item is sold.

3. It is possible to apply the lower of cost or market basis to each item in the inventory, major classes or categories, or the inventory as a whole.

4. The method elected for inventory valuation (cost, or lower of cost or market) must be followed consistently from year to year.

C. Obsolete, spoiled, or damaged merchandise and other merchandise that can only be sold at prices below cost should be valued at net realizable value. Net realizable value is the estimated selling price less any direct cost of disposition, such as sales commissions.

VII. Accounting For and Reporting Inventory Under a Perpetual System.
  A. The use of a perpetual inventory system for merchandise provides the most effective means of control over inventory. Although it is possible to maintain a perpetual inventory in the memorandum records only or to limit the inventory to quantities, a complete set of records integrated with the general ledger is preferable. Through the use of computers, integrated perpetual inventory systems are being used by more and more companies.
  B. Under the perpetual inventory system, all merchandise increases and decreases are recorded in a manner similar to the recording of increases and decreases in cash. The merchandise inventory account at any point in time reflects the merchandise on hand at that date.
  C. The basic accounting entries for a perpetual inventory system are as follows:
    1. Purchases of merchandise are recorded by debiting Merchandise Inventory and crediting Accounts Payable or Cash.
    2. Sales of merchandise are recorded by debiting Cost of Merchandise Sold and crediting Merchandise Inventory.
    3. Unlike the periodic inventory system, no adjusting journal entries are necessary for beginning and ending inventory under the perpetual inventory system.
    4. The balance in the merchandise inventory account as of the end of the accounting period would be the amount reported on the balance sheet on that date.
    5. The balance of the cost of merchandise sold account would be the amount reported on the income statement for the period.
VIII. Inventory Costing Methods Under a Perpetual System.
  A. Under a perpetual inventory system, details of the inventory transactions are maintained in a subsidiary inventory ledger. Whether this ledger is computerized or maintained manually, it is customary to use one of three costing methods (first-in, first-out; last-in, first-out; or average).
  B. Under the first-in, first-out method of cost flow in a perpetual system, the number of units sold and number of units on hand after each transaction are accounted for on the fifo basis. The items received first are assumed to be the first sold.
  C. Under the last-in, first-out method of cost flow in a perpetual system, the number of units sold and the number of units on hand after each transaction are accounted for on the last-in, first-out basis. The items received last are assumed to be the first sold.
  D. When the average cost method is used in a perpetual inventory system, an average unit cost for each type of commodity is computed each time a purchase is made. Sometimes this averaging technique is called a moving average.
IX. Internal Control and Perpetual Inventory Systems.
  A. The basic control feature of a perpetual inventory system is the recording of all merchandise transactions (increases and decreases) as each transaction occurs. The balance of the merchandise inventory account shows the amount of inventory on hand at any given point in time. A comparison of the recorded (book) inventory with the physical quantities on hand can be used to determine the existence and seriousness of any inventory shortages.
  B. The subsidiary inventory ledger can aid in maintaining inventory quantities at an optimal level by facilitating the timely reordering of merchandise and the avoidance of excess inventory.
X. Automated Perpetual Inventory Records.
  A. If there is a large number of inventory items and/or transactions, businesses will often computerize the perpetual system for faster and more accurate processing of data.
  B. By computerizing a system, additional data may be entered into the inventory records so that inventory may be ordered and maintained at optimum levels.
XI. Presentation of Merchandise Inventory on the Balance Sheet.
  A. Merchandise inventory is usually presented on the balance sheet immediately following receivables.
  B. Both the method of determining the cost of the inventory (fifo, lifo, or average) and the method of valuing the inventory (cost, or lower of cost or market) should be shown. The details may be disclosed by a parenthetical notation or a footnote.
XII. Estimating Inventory Cost.
  A. In practice, an inventory amount may be needed to prepare an income statement when it is impractical or impossible to take a physical inventory or to maintain perpetual inventory records. In such cases, inventory estimation methods may be used.
  B. The retail method of estimating inventory costs is based on the relationship of the cost of merchandise available for sale to the retail price of the same merchandise.
    1. The retail prices of all merchandise acquired are accumulated in supplementary records.
    2. The inventory at retail is determined by deducting sales for the period from the retail price of the goods that were available for sale during the period.

3. The inventory at retail is then converted to cost on the basis of the ratio of cost to selling (retail) price for the merchandise available for sale.

4. An inherent assumption in the retail method of inventory estimation is that the composition or "mix" of the commodities in the ending inventory, in terms of percent of cost to selling price, is comparable to the entire stock of merchandise available for sale.

5. One of the major advantages of the retail method is that it provides inventory figures for interim statements.

6. The retail method can be used in conjunction with the periodic system when a physical inventory is taken at the end of the year.

C. The gross profit method of estimating inventory costs uses an estimate of the gross profit realized during the period to estimate the inventory at the end of the period.

1. Merchandise available for sale is accumulated in the accounting records.

2. An estimate of gross profit percentage is multiplied by the sales for the period to determine the estimated cost of merchandise sold.

3. Estimated inventory is then determined by subtracting from the merchandise available for sale the estimated cost of merchandise sold for the period.

4. The estimate of the gross profit rate is ordinarily based on the actual rate for the preceding year, adjusted for any changes made in the cost and sales prices during the current period.

5. The gross profit method may be used in estimating the cost of merchandise destroyed by fire or other disaster, or in preparing interim statements.

PART 1

Instructions: A list of terms and related statements appear below. From the list of terms, select the one that relates to each statement and print its identifying letter in the space provided.

A. Average cost method
B. First-in, first-out (fifo) method
C. Gross profit method
D. Last-in, first-out (lifo) method

E. Lower of cost or market
F. Merchandise inventory
G. Net realizable value
H. Periodic inventory system

I. Perpetual inventory system
J. Retail inventory method

_____ 1. The inventory of merchandise purchased for resale is commonly called (?)

_____ 2. An inventory system in which only the revenue from sales is recorded each time a sale is made.

_____ 3. An inventory system in which both the revenue and cost of sales are recorded each time a sale is made.

_____ 4. An inventory costing method that treats the first merchandise acquired as the first merchandise sold.

_____ 5. An inventory costing method in which the ending inventory is assumed to be composed of the earliest costs.

_____ 6. An inventory costing method in which the weighted average unit costs are used in determining both ending inventory and cost of goods sold.

_____ 7. A method of inventory pricing in which goods are valued at original cost or replacement cost, whichever is lower.

_____ 8. The estimated selling price of inventory less any direct cost of disposition.

_____ 9. An inventory method based on the relationship of the cost of merchandise available for sale to the retail price of the same merchandise.

_____ 10. An inventory method which uses an estimate of the gross profit realized during the period to estimate the inventory at the end of the period.

Name _____

PART 2

Instructions: Indicate whether each of the following statements is true or false by placing a check mark in the appropriate column.

	True	False
1. If merchandise inventory at the end of the period is understated, gross profit will be overstated . .	____	____
2. The two principal systems of inventory accounting are periodic and physical	____	____
3. When terms of a sale are FOB destination, title usually does not pass to the buyer until the commodities are delivered	____	____
4. Without the use of a computer, specific identification inventory procedures are usually too costly and too time consuming to justify their use	____	____
5. During a period of rising prices, the inventory costing method which will result in the highest amount of net income is fifo	____	____
6. If the cost of units purchased and the prices at which they were sold remain stable, all three inventory methods will yield the same results	____	____
7. When the rate of inflation is high, the larger gross profits that result are frequently called inventory profits.	____	____
8. As used in the phrase lower of cost or market, "market" means selling price	____	____
9. When the retail inventory method is used, inventory at retail is converted to cost on the basis of the ratio of cost to replacement cost of the merchandise available for sale	____	____
10. Merchandise inventory is usually presented on the balance sheet immediately following receivables	____	____

PART 3

Instructions: Complete each of the following statements by circling the letter of the best answer.

1. If merchandise inventory at the end of the period is overstated,
   a. gross profit will be understated
   b. owner's equity will be overstated
   c. net income will be understated
   d. cost of merchandise sold will be overstated

2. If merchandise inventory at the end of period 1 is understated, and at the end of period 2 is correct,
   a. gross profit in period 2 will be overstated
   b. assets at the end of period 2 will be overstated
   c. owner's equity at the end of period 2 will be understated
   d. cost of merchandise sold in period 2 will be overstated

3. During a period of rising prices, the inventory costing method which will result in the lowest amount of net income is
   a. fifo
   b. lifo
   c. average cost
   d. perpetual

4. If the replacement price of an item of inventory is lower than its cost, the use of the lower of cost or market method
   a. is not permitted unless a perpetual inventory system is maintained
   b. is recommended in order to maximize the reported net income
   c. tends to overstate the gross profit
   d. reduces gross profit for the period in which the decline occurred

5. When lifo is strictly applied to a perpetual inventory system, the unit cost prices assigned to the ending inventory will not necessarily be those associated with the earliest unit costs of the period if
   a. a physical inventory is taken at the end of the period
   b. physical inventory records are maintained throughout the period in terms of quantities only
   c. at any time during a period the number of units of a commodity sold exceeds the number previously purchased during the same period
   d. moving average inventory cost is maintained

PART 4

Han Co. is a small wholesaler of fashion luggage. The accounting records show the following purchases and sales of the Style 80 Suburban during the first year of business.

STYLE 80 SUBURBAN

Purchases				Sales	
Date	Units	Price	Total Cost	Date	Units
Jan. 20	45	$ 71	$ 3,195	Feb. 15	40
Apr. 10	70	85	5,950	Apr. 20	50
Aug. 5	30	110	3,300	Aug. 24	35
Dec. 21	55	125	6,875	Dec. 27	15
Total	200		$19,320		140

A physical count of Style 80 at the end of the year reveals that 60 are still on hand.

Instructions: (1) Determine the cost of Style 80 inventory as of December 31 by means of the average cost method with a periodic system:

Average unit cost   = $ _____   = $ _____

_____ units in the inventory   @ $ _____   = $ _____

(2) Determine the cost of Style 80 inventory as of December 31 by means of the first-in, first-out (fifo) method with a periodic system:

INVENTORY (Fifo Periodic)

Date Purchased	Units	Price	Total Cost

(3) Determine the cost of Style 80 inventory as of December 31 by means of the last-in, first-out (lifo) method with a periodic inventory system:

INVENTORY (Lifo Periodic)

Date Purchased	Units	Price	Total Cost

(4) Determine the cost of Style 80 inventory as of December 31 by means of the last-in, first-out (lifo) method with a perpetual inventory system:

INVENTORY (Lifo Perpetual)

Date Purchased	Units	Price	Total Cost

Helfrich Co. began operating on January 1, 1987. During 1987, Helfrich sold 23,000 units at an average price of $80 each, and made the following purchases:

Date of Purchase	Units	Unit Price	Total Cost
January 1	5,400	$44	$ 237,600
March 1	4,100	48	196,800
June 1	4,800	55	264,000
September 1	7,400	63	466,200
November 1	4,400	70	308,000
December 1	1,900	75	142,500
	28,000		$1,615,100

Instructions: Determine the ending inventory, the cost of merchandise sold, and the gross profit for Helfrich, using each of the following methods of inventory costing: **(1)** fifo, **(2)** lifo, and **(3)** average cost. (Round unit cost to two decimal places.)

	(1) Fifo	(2) Lifo	(3) Average Cost
Sales	$ _____	$ _____	$ _____
Purchases.................................	$1,615,100	$1,615,100	$1,615,100
Less ending inventory	_____	_____	_____
Cost of merchandise sold	$ _____	$ _____	$ _____
Gross profit...............................	$ _____	$ _____	$ _____

PART 6

Instructions: Complete the following summary, which illustrates the application of the lower of cost or market rule to individual inventory items of Leminger Company.

Description	Quantity	Unit Cost Price	Unit Market Price	Total Cost	Total Lower of C or M
Commodity A	750	$4.00	$3.60	$ _____	$ _____
Commodity B......................................	500	7.25	7.50	_____	_____
Commodity C......................................	450	5.90	5.50	_____	_____
Commodity D	200	5.00	4.50	_____	_____
Total				$ _____	$ _____

PART 7

Cash Inc. operates a department store and takes a physical inventory at the end of each calendar year. However, Cash likes to have a balance sheet and an income statement available at the end of each month in order to study financial position and operating trends. Cash estimates inventory at the end of each month for accounting statement preparation purposes. The following information is available as of January 31 of the current year:

	Cost	Retail
Merchandise inventory, January 1	$123,600	$172,000
Purchases in January	269,000	480,600
Purchases returns and allowances—January	5,000	6,600
Sales in January		495,000
Sales returns and allowances—January		11,000

Instructions: (1) Determine the estimated cost of the inventory on January 31, using the retail method.

	Cost	Retail
Merchandise inventory, January 1	$_____	$_____
Purchases in January (net)	_____	_____
Merchandise available for sale	$_____	$_____

Ratio of cost to retail:

$$\frac{\$\text{_____}}{\$\text{_____}} = \quad \% $$

Sales in January (net)	_____
Merchandise inventory, January 31, at retail	$_____

Merchandise inventory, January 31, at estimated cost ($_____ ×

____%) .... $_____

(2) Determine the estimated cost of inventory on January 31, using the gross profit method. On the basis of past experience, Cash estimates a rate of gross profit of 36% of net sales.

Merchandise inventory, January 1	$_____
Purchases in January (net)	_____
Merchandise available for sale	$_____
Sales in January (net)	$_____
Less estimated gross profit ($_____ × ____%)	_____
Estimated cost of merchandise sold	_____
Estimated merchandise inventory, January 31	$_____

Page not used

Chapter 11

PLANT ASSETS AND INTANGIBLE ASSETS

STUDY GOALS

After studying this chapter, you should be able to:
1. List the characteristics of plant assets and prepare journal entries for the acquisition of plant assets.
2. Explain the nature of depreciation and prepare journal entries for the recording of depreciation.
3. Prepare journal entries for accounting for plant disposals.
4. List the methods of accounting for leasing of plant assets and prepare journal entries for the operating lease method.
5. Explain the nature of depletion and prepare journal entries for the recording of depletion.
6. List the characteristics of intangible assets and prepare journal entries for the recording of intangible assets.
7. Prepare financial statement presentations for depreciation expense, plant assets, and intangible assets.

GLOSSARY OF KEY TERMS

Accelerated depreciation method. A depreciation method that provides for a high depreciation charge in the first year of use of an asset and gradually declining periodic charges thereafter.

Amortization. The periodic expense attributed to the decline in usefulness of an intangible asset.

Boot. The balance owed the supplier when an old asset is traded for a new asset.

Capital expenditure. A cost that adds to the utility of an asset for more than one accounting period.

Capital lease. A lease which includes one or more of four provisions that result in treating the leased asset as a purchased asset in the accounts.

Composite-rate depreciation method. A method of depreciation based on the use of a single rate that applies to entire groups of assets.

Declining-balance depreciation method. A method of depreciation that provides declining periodic depreciation charges to expense over the estimated life of an asset.

Depletion. The cost of metal ores and other minerals removed from the earth.

Depreciation. The decrease in usefulness of all plant assets except land.

Goodwill. An intangible asset that attaches to a business as a result of such favorable factors as location,
product superiority, reputation, and managerial skill.

Intangible asset. A long-lived asset that is useful in the operations of an enterprise, is not held for sale, and is without physical qualities.

Operating lease. A lease which does not meet the criteria for a capital lease, and thus which is accounted for as an operating expense, so that neither future lease obligations nor future rights to use the leased asset are recognized in the accounts.

Plant asset. A tangible asset of a relatively fixed or permanent nature owned by a business enterprise.

Residual value. The estimated recoverable cost of a depreciable asset as of the time of its removal from service.

Revenue expenditure. An expenditure that benefits only the current period.

Straight-line depreciation method. A method of depreciation that provides for equal periodic charges to expense over the estimated life of an asset.

Sum-of-the-years-digits depreciation method. A method of depreciation that provides for declining periodic depreciation charges to expense over the estimated life of an asset.

Units-of-production depreciation method. A method of depreciation that provides for depreciation expense based on the expected productive capacity of an asset.

CHAPTER OUTLINE

I. Initial Costs of Plant Assets.
   A. Plant assets are assets which are tangible in nature, used in the operations of the business, and are not held for sale in the ordinary course of business. Other descriptive titles frequently used are fixed assets and property, plant, and equipment.
   B. The initial cost of a plant asset includes all expenditures necessary to get it in place and ready for use. Such expenditures include sales taxes, transportation charges, insurance, etc.
   C. The cost of constructing a building includes the fees paid to architects and engineers for plans and supervision, insurance, etc. Interest incurred during the construction period on money borrowed to finance construction should also be included in the cost of the building.
   D. The cost of land includes not only the negotiated price but also broker's commissions, title fees, surveying fees, etc. If delinquent real estate taxes are assumed by the buyer, they are also chargeable to the land.
   E. Expenditures for improvements that are neither as permanent as land nor directly associated with the building may be set apart in a land improvements account and depreciated accordingly. Such items include trees and shrubs, fences, and paved parking areas.

II. Nature of Depreciation.
   A. As time passes, all plant assets with the exception of land lose their capacity to yield services. Accordingly, the cost of such assets should be transferred to the related expense accounts through depreciation.
   B. Factors contributing to a decline in usefulness of an asset may be divided into two categories: physical depreciation, which includes wear from use and deterioration from the action of the elements, and functional depreciation, which includes inadequacy and obsolescence.
   C. The meaning of the term "depreciation" as used in accounting may be misunderstood because depreciation is not necessarily associated with declines in the market value of an asset. In addition, depreciation does not provide cash for the replacement of assets.

III. Determining Depreciation.
   A. In determining periodic depreciation expense, three factors need to be considered: the plant asset's (a) initial cost, (b) residual value, and (c) useful life. The residual value and useful life of the plant asset must be estimated relying upon such factors as frequency of use, maintenance, etc.
   B. The straight-line method of determining depreciation provides for equal periodic charges to expense over the estimated life of the asset.
      1. The depreciable cost of the asset is determined by subtracting the estimated residual value from the initial cost of the asset.
      2. The useful life of the asset is then divided into the depreciable cost.
      3. The resulting amount is an annual depreciation charge which remains constant over the life of the asset.
      4. Straight-line depreciation is often expressed by a percentage rate. The straight-line depreciation rate is equal to 100 divided by the useful life of the asset.
      5. The straight-line method is widely used because of its simplicity.
   C. The units-of-production method yields a depreciation charge that varies with the amount of asset usage.
      1. The depreciable cost of the asset is determined by subtracting the estimated residual value from the initial cost of the asset.
      2. The estimated life of the asset, expressed in terms of machine hours or direct labor hours, is then divided into the depreciable cost to arrive at the unit or hourly depreciation charge.
      3. The actual amount of production usage is then multiplied by this rate to determine the depreciation charge.
      4. The amount of depreciation will depend upon the asset usage and will normally vary from year to year.
   D. The declining-balance method yields a declining periodic depreciation charge over the estimated life of the asset.
      1. The double-declining balance method uses a rate of depreciation which is double the straight-line depreciation rate.
      2. The declining-balance depreciation rate is then applied to the original cost of the asset for the first year, and thereafter to the book value (cost minus accumulated depreciation).
      3. The residual value of the asset is not considered in determining the depreciation rate or the depreciation charge each period, except that the book value of the asset should not be allowed to depreciate below the estimated residual value.
   E. The sum-of-the-years-digits method yields depreciation results which are similar to those of the declining-balance method.
      1. The depreciable cost of the asset is deter-

mined by subtracting the estimated residual value from the initial cost of the asset.

2. The depreciation rate per year is determined by a fraction, of which the numerator is the number of years of remaining life at the beginning of the year and the denominator is the sum of the years of useful life.

3. The depreciation charge for the period is determined by multiplying the sum-of-the-years-digits rate by the depreciable cost of the asset.

4. This method yields depreciation charges which decline over the life of the asset.

F. If the first use of the asset does not coincide with the beginning of the fiscal year, depreciation should be allocated for the first partial year of use.

G. Business entities may choose among depreciation methods for financial statement reporting purposes.

1. The straight-line method provides uniform periodic charges to depreciation expense over the life of the asset.

2. The units-of-production method provides for periodic charges to depreciation expense that may vary considerably depending upon the amount of use of the asset.

3. Both the declining-balance and sum-of-the-years-digits methods provide for a higher depreciation charge in the first year of use of the asset and a gradually declining periodic charge thereafter. For this reason, these methods are referred to as accelerated depreciation methods.

4. The accelerated depreciation methods are most appropriate for situations in which the decline in productivity or earning power of the asset is proportionately greater in the early years of its use than in later years. Justification for accelerated depreciation methods is provided by the tendency of repairs to increase with the age of the asset.

IV. Depreciation for Federal Income Tax.

A. Each of the four depreciation methods described in the preceding paragraphs can be used to determine the amount of depreciation for federal income tax purposes for plant assets acquired prior to 1981.

B. For plant assets acquired after 1980 and before 1987, either the straight-line method or the Accelerated Cost Recovery System (ACRS) may be used to determine depreciation deductions for federal income tax purposes.

C. The Tax Reform Act of 1986 revised ACRS by providing for 8 classes of useful life for plant assets acquired after 1986. The depreciation deduction for the two most common classes — the 5-year class (automobiles and

light-duty trucks) and the 7-year class (most machinery and equipment) — approximates the use of the 200-percent declining-balance method.

V. Revision of Periodic Depreciation.

A. In determining periodic depreciation, estimated useful lives and residual values are utilized.

B. Changes in these estimates are accounted for by using the revised estimates to determine the amount of remaining undepreciable asset cost to be charged as an expense in future periods.

C. The correction of minor errors in the estimates used in the determination of depreciation does not affect the amounts of depreciation expense recorded in earlier years.

VI. Recording Depreciation.

A. Depreciation may be recorded by an entry at the end of each month, or the adjustment may be delayed until the end of the year.

B. Depreciation is recorded by using a contra asset account, Accumulated Depreciation, or Allowance for Depreciation, so that the original cost of the asset may be reported along with the accumulated depreciation to date. This reporting is required for property tax and income tax purposes, as well as financial statement purposes.

C. An exception to the general procedure of recording depreciation monthly or annually is made when a plant asset is sold, traded in, or scrapped, in which case depreciation must be brought up to date as of the date the asset is disposed of.

VII. Capital and Revenue Expenditures.

A. Expenditures for additions to plant assets or expenditures that add to the utility of assets for more than one accounting period are called capital expenditures.

1. Expenditures for an addition to a plant asset should be debited to the plant asset account.

2. Expenditures that increase operating efficiency or capacity for the remaining useful life of a plant asset should be debited to the plant asset account.

3. Expenditures that increase the useful life of the asset beyond the original estimate are debited to the appropriate accumulated depreciation account.

B. Expenditures that benefit only the current period and that are made in order to maintain normal operating efficiency of plant assets are called revenue expenditures.

1. Expenditures for ordinary maintenance and repairs of a recurring nature are revenue expenditures and should be debited to expense accounts.

2. Small expenditures are usually treated as repair expense, even though they may

have characteristics of capital expenditures. The saving in time and clerical expenses justifies the sacrifice of the small degree of accuracy.

VIII. Disposal of Plant Assets.

A. A plant asset should not be removed from the accounts only because it has been depreciated for the full period of its estimated life. If the asset is still useful to the enterprise, the cost and accumulated depreciation should remain in the ledger. In this way, accountability for the asset is maintained.

B. When plant assets are no longer useful to the business and have no market value, they are discarded.
   1. If the asset has been fully depreciated, then no loss is realized.
   2. The entry to record the disposal of a fully depreciated asset with no market value is to debit Accumulated Depreciation and credit the asset account.
   3. If the asset is not fully depreciated, depreciation should be brought up to date before the accumulated depreciation account is debited. The difference between the cost of the plant asset and its accumulated depreciation (book value) is recognized as a loss.
   4. Losses and gains on disposals of plant assets are nonoperating items and may be reported in the Other Expense or Other Income section of the income statement.

C. The entry to record the sale of a plant asset is similar to the entry to record the disposal of a plant asset as set forth above.
   1. The first entry should be to update the depreciation expense for the period.
   2. The cash received from the sale of the plant asset should be recorded.
   3. The accumulated depreciation account should be debited for its balance, and the plant asset account should be credited for its cost. Any difference in the debits and credits to balance the entry will be reported as a gain (credit) or loss (debit) on the sale of the plant asset.

D. Plant assets may be traded in for new equipment having a similar use.
   1. The trade-in allowance is deducted from the price of the new equipment. The balance owed is paid according to credit terms and is called boot.
   2. If the trade-in allowance is less than the book value of the old plant asset, the loss on the trade-in is recognized immediately.
   3. If the trade-in value of the plant asset is greater than its book value, the gain is not recognized for financial reporting purposes. Instead, the amount of the gain is deducted from the cost of the new equipment. In effect, this gain is recognized over the life of the new asset as a reduction in the periodic depreciation charges which would otherwise be recognized.
   4. The Internal Revenue Code requires that neither gains nor losses be recognized on trade-ins of assets of similar use. Any gain or loss on the exchange is treated as a reduction in or addition to the cost of the new asset acquired.

IX. Subsidiary Ledgers for Plant Assets.

A. When depreciation is to be computed individually on a large number of assets making up a functional group, it is advisable to maintain a subsidiary ledger.

B. The sum of the asset balances and the sum of the accumulated depreciation balances in all of the accounts should be compared periodically with the balances of their respective controlling accounts in the general ledger.

C. Subsidiary ledgers for plant assets are useful to the accounting department in:
   1. Determining the periodic depreciation expense.
   2. Recording the disposal of individual items.
   3. Preparing tax returns.
   4. Preparing insurance claims in the event of insured losses.

D. Regardless of whether subsidiary equipment ledgers are maintained, plant assets should be inspected periodically in order to determine their state of repair and whether or not they are still in use.

X. Composite-Rate Depreciation Method.

A. The composite-rate depreciation method determines depreciation for entire groups of assets by use of a single rate. The basis for grouping may be similarity in life estimates or other common traits.

B. When depreciation is computed on the basis of a composite group of assets of differing life spans, a rate based on averages must be developed using the following procedures:
   1. The annual depreciation for each asset is computed.
   2. The total annual depreciation is determined for the group of assets.
   3. The total annual depreciation divided by the total cost of the assets determines the composite rate.

C. Although new assets of differing life spans and residual values will be added to the group of assets and old assets will be retired, the "mix" of assets is assumed to remain relatively unchanged.

D. When a composite rate is used, it may be applied against total asset cost on a monthly basis, or some reasonable assumption may be made regarding the timing of increases and decreases in the group. A common practice is to assume that all additions and retirements have occurred uniformly throughout the year.

E. When assets within the composite group are retired, no gain or loss should be recognized. Instead, the asset account is credited for the cost of the asset and the accumulated depreciation account is debited for the excess of cost over the amount realized from the disposal.

F. Regardless of whether depreciation is computed for each individual unit or for composite groups, the periodic depreciation charge is based upon estimates.

XI. Depreciation of Plant Assets of Low Unit Cost.

A. Subsidiary ledgers are not usually maintained for classes of plant assets that are made up of individual items of low unit cost. In such cases, the usual depreciation methods are not practical.

B. One common method of determining cost expiration is to take a periodic inventory of the items on hand, estimate their fair value based on original cost, and transfer the remaining amount from the asset account to an appropriately titled expense account. Such categories of assets include tools, dies, molds, patterns, and spare parts.

XII. Acquisition of Plant Assets Through Leasing.

A. Instead of owning a plant asset, a business may acquire the use of a plant asset through a lease.

1. A lease is a contractual agreement that conveys the right to use an asset for a stated period of time.

2. The two parties to a lease are the lessor (the party who legally owns the asset and who conveys the rights to use the asset to the lessee) and the lessee (the party that leases the asset for its use).

B. Capital leases are defined as leases that include one or more of the following provisions:

1. The lease transfers ownership of the leased asset to the lessee at the end of the lease term.

2. The lease contains an option for a bargain purchase of the leased asset by the lessee.

3. The lease term extends over most of the economic life of the leased asset.

4. The lease requires rental payments which approximate the fair market value of the leased asset.

C. Leases which do not meet the preceding criteria for capital leases are classified as operating leases.

D. A capital lease is accounted for as if the lessee has, in fact, purchased the asset. The lessee will debit an asset account for the fair market value of a leased asset and credit a long-term lease liability account.

E. In accounting for operating leases, rent expense is recognized as the leased asset is used.

F. Financial reporting disclosures require the presentation of future lease commitments in footnotes to the financial statements.

XIII. Depletion.

A. The periodic allocation of the cost of metal ores and other minerals removed from the earth is called depletion.

B. The amount of periodic cost allocation (depletion expense) reported each period is based on the relationship of the cost to the estimated size of the mineral deposit and on the quantity extracted during the particular period.

C. The adjusting entry for depletion is a debit to Depletion Expense and a credit to Accumulated Depletion. The accumulated depletion account is a contra account to the asset to which the cost of the mineral deposit was initially recorded.

XIV. Intangible Assets.

A. Long-lived assets that are useful in the operations of an enterprise, not held for sale, and without physical qualities are classified as intangible assets.

1. The basic principles of accounting for intangible assets are like those described earlier for plant assets.

2. The major accounting issues involving intangible assets are the determination of the initial costs and the recognition of periodic cost expiration, called amortization, due to the passage of time or a decline in usefulness of the intangible asset.

3. Intangible assets often include patents, copyrights, and goodwill.

B. Patents provide exclusive rights to produce and sell goods with one or more unique features.

1. Patents are granted by the federal government and continue in effect for 17 years.

2. An enterprise may obtain patents on new products developed in its own research laboratories or it may purchase patent rights from others.

3. The initial cost of a purchased patent should be debited to an asset account and then written off, or amortized, over the years of its expected usefulness.

4. The straight-line method of amortization should be used unless it can be shown that another method is more appropriate.

5. A separate contra asset account is normally not credited for the write-off of patent amortization and the credit is recorded directly to the patent account.

6. Current accounting principles require that research and development costs expended in the development of patents should be

written off as incurred.

7. Legal fees related to patent purchase or development should be recognized and amortized over the useful life of the patent.

C. The exclusive right to publish and sell a literary, artistic, or musical composition is obtained by a copyright.

1. Copyrights are issued by the federal government and extend for 50 years beyond the author's death.

2. The costs assigned to a copyright include all costs of creating the work plus the cost of obtaining the copyright.

3. A copyright that is purchased from another should be recorded at the price paid for it.

4. Copyrights should be amortized over their useful lives.

D. Goodwill is an intangible asset that attaches to a business as a result of such favorable factors as location, product superiority, reputation, and managerial skill.

1. Goodwill should be recognized in the accounts only if it can be objectively deter-

mined by an event or transaction, such as the purchase or sale of a business.

2. Goodwill should be amortized over the years of its useful life, which should not exceed 40 years.

XV. Reporting Depreciation Expense, Plant Assets, and Intangible Assets in the Financial Statements.

A. The amount of depreciation expense or amortization should be set forth separately in the income statement or disclosed in some other manner.

B. A general description of the method or methods used in computing depreciation or amortization should also accompany the financial statements.

C. The balance of each major class of depreciable assets should be disclosed in the balance sheet or in notes thereto, together with the related accumulated depreciation, either by major class or in total.

D. Intangible assets are usually presented in the balance sheet in a separate section immediately following plant assets.

PART 1

Instructions: A list of terms and related statements appear below. From the list of terms, select the one that relates to each statement and print its identifying letter in the space provided.

A. Amortization   **E.** Declining-balance method   **H.** Residual value
B. Boot   **F.** Depletion   **I.** Revenue expenditures
C. Capital   **G.** Depreciation   **J.** Straight-line method
D. Capital expenditures

_____ 1. The allocation of the cost of a plant asset to expense over its expected useful life.

_____ 2. The estimated value of a plant asset at the time that it is to be retired from service.

_____ 3. A method of depreciation which provides for equal periodic charges to expense over the estimated life of the asset.

_____ 4. A method of depreciation which yields a declining periodic depreciation charge over the estimated life of the asset.

_____ 5. Expenditures that add to the utility of the asset for more than one accounting period.

_____ 6. Expenditures that benefit only the current period, and that are made in order to maintain normal operating efficiency.

_____ 7. The balance owed after the trade-in allowance is deducted from the price of new equipment acquired in a trade for equipment having similar uses.

_____ 8. A lease which is accounted for as if the lessee has purchased the asset is called a (?) lease.

_____ 9. The periodic allocation of the cost of natural resources to expense as the units are removed.

_____10. The allocation to expense of the cost of an intangible asset over the periods of its economic usefulness.

PART 2

Instructions: Indicate whether each of the following statements is true or false by placing a check mark in the appropriate column.

	True	False
1. The decline in usefulness of a plant asset because of wear from use and deterioration from the action of the elements is called functional depreciation.	____	____
2. The method of depreciation which yields a depreciation charge that varies with the amount of asset usage is known as the units-of-production method.	____	____
3. The method of depreciation that, each year of an asset's estimated life, applies a successively smaller fraction to the original cost less the estimated residual value is called the declining-balance method.	____	____
4. In using the declining-balance method, the asset should not be depreciated below the net book value.	____	____
5. Accelerated depreciation methods are most appropriate for situations in which the decline in productivity or earning power of the asset is proportionately greater in the early years of its use than in later years.	____	____
6. ACRS depreciation methods permit the use of asset lives that are often much shorter than the actual useful life.	____	____
7. When an old plant asset is traded in for a new plant asset having a similar use, proper accounting treatment prohibits recognition of a loss.	____	____
8. A procedure to determine depreciation for entire groups of assets by use of a single rate is called the composite-rate depreciation method.	____	____
9. A lease which transfers ownership of the leased asset to the lessee at the end of the lease term should be classified as an operating lease.	____	____
10. Long-lived assets that are useful in the operations of an enterprise, not held for sale, and without physical qualities are usually classified as intangible assets.	____	____

PART 3

Instructions: Complete each of the following statements by circling the letter of the best answer.

1. If unwanted buildings are located on land acquired for a plant site, the cost of their removal, less any salvage recovered, should be charged to the
   a. expense accounts
   b. building account
   c. land account
   d. accumulated depreciation account

2. The depreciation method used most often in the financial statements is the
   a. straight-line method
   b. declining-balance method
   c. units-of-production method
   d. sum-of-the-years-digits method

3. The depreciation method that would provide the highest reported net income in the early years of an asset's life would be
   a. straight-line
   b. declining-balance
   c. sum-of-the-years-digits
   d. accelerated

4. Equipment with an estimated useful life of 4 years and an estimated residual value of $600 is acquired at a cost of $11,000. Using the sum-of-the-years-digits method, what is the amount of depreciation for the first year of use of the equipment?
   a. $2,080
   b. $2,200
   c. $4,160
   d. $4,400

5. Equipment that cost $20,000 was originally estimated to have a useful life of 8 years and a residual value of $2,000. The equipment has been depreciated for 4 years using straight-line depreciation. During the fifth year it is estimated that the remaining useful life is 6 years (instead of 4) and that the residual value is $1,000 (instead of $2,000). The depreciation expense on the equipment in year 5 using the straight-line method would be
   a. $2,250
   b. $1,333
   c. $1,800
   d. $1,667

6. Assume that a drill press is rebuilt during its sixth year of use, so that its useful life is extended 5 years beyond the original estimate of 10 years. In this case, the cost of rebuilding the drill press should be charged to the appropriate
   a. expense account
   b. accumulated depreciation account
   c. asset account
   d. liability account

7. Old equipment which cost $8,000 and has accumulated depreciation of $6,500 is given, along with $12,000 in cash, for the same type of new equipment with a price of $15,200. At what amount should the new equipment be recorded?
   a. $15,200
   b. $13,700
   c. $13,500
   d. $12,000

8. Assume the same facts as in No. 7, except that the old equipment and $14,000 in cash is given for the new equipment. At what amount should the new equipment be recorded for financial accounting purposes?
   a. $15,500
   b. $15,200
   c. $14,000
   d. $13,700

9. In a lease contract, the party who legally owns the asset is the
   a. contractor
   b. operator
   c. lessee
   d. lessor

10. Which of the following items is not considered an intangible asset?
    a. land
    b. patent
    c. copyright
    d. goodwill

PART 4

Bowman Inc. is planning to trade in its present truck for a new model on June 30 of the current year. The existing truck was purchased July 1 four years ago at a cost of $15,000, and accumulated depreciation is $12,000 through June 30 of the current year. The new truck has a list price of $21,500. Bryant Motors agrees to allow Bowman $3,100 for the present truck, and Bowman agrees to pay the balance of $18,400 in cash.

Instructions: Record the exchange according to acceptable methods of accounting for exchanges. (Omit explanation.)

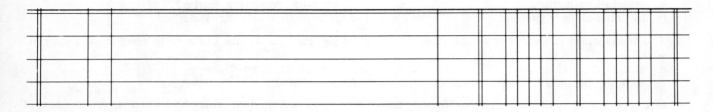

PART 5

Assume the same facts as in Part 4, except that the allowance on the present truck is $800 and that Bowman agrees to pay the balance of $20,700 in cash.

Instructions: (1) Record the exchange according to acceptable methods of accounting for exchanges.

(2) Record the exchange as in (1), except that the entry should be in conformity with the requirements of the Internal Revenue Code.

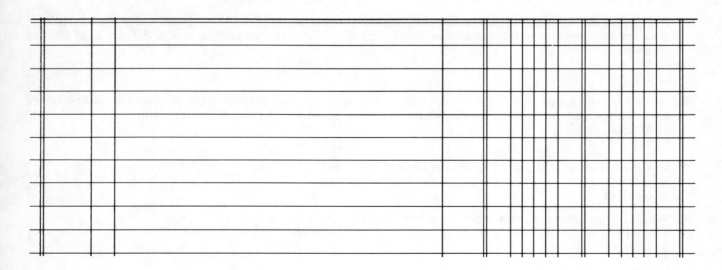

130

PART 6

Burns Inc. has a sales representative who must travel a substantial amount. A car for this purpose was acquired January 2 four years ago at a cost of $12,000. It is estimated to have a total useful life of 4 years.

Instructions: (1) Record the annual depreciation on Burns' car at the end of the first and fourth years of ownership, using the straight-line method and assuming no salvage value. (Omit explanation.)

(2) Record the annual depreciation on Burns' car at the end of the first and fourth years of ownership, using the declining-balance method at twice the straight-line rate. (Omit explanation.)

(3) Record the annual depreciation on Burns' car at the end of the first and fourth years of ownership, using the sum-of-the-years-digits method and assuming no salvage value. (Omit explanation.)

PART 7

Berry Inc. uses a composite rate of 20% for the depreciation of several pieces of equipment, based on the total of the annual depreciation charges on these assets divided by their total cost. Assuming that the balance of the equipment account at the end of the current year is $18,000 and that all of the equipment has been in use throughout the entire year, record the depreciation of Berry's equipment. (Omit explanation.)

PART 8

Fettinger Inc. uses the units-of-production method for computing depreciation on its machines. One machine, which cost $74,800, is estimated to have a useful life of 22,000 hours and no residual value. During the first year of operation, this machine was used a total of 4,200 hours. Record the depreciation of this machine at the end of the first year. (Omit explanation.)

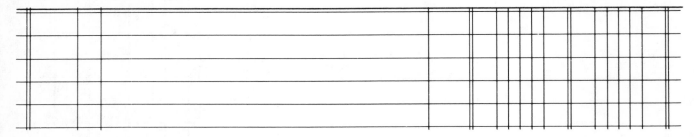

PART 9

On April 6, Kevin's Hardware Emporium decides to sell for $1,800 cash some fixtures for which it paid $6,700 and on which it has taken total depreciation of $5,450 to date of sale. Record this sale. (Omit explanation.)

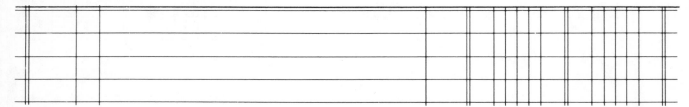

PART 10

Grannan Co. paid $1,061,500 for some mineral rights in Arizona. The deposit is estimated to contain 550,000 tons of ore of uniform grade. Record the depletion of this deposit at the end of the first year, assuming that 50,000 tons are mined during the year. (Omit explanation.)

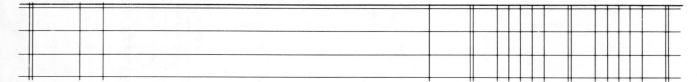

PART 11

Leminger Racing Inc. acquires a patent at the beginning of its calendar (fiscal) year for $111,000. Although the patent will not expire for another twelve years, it is expected to be of value for only six years. Record the amortization of this patent at the end of the fiscal year. (Omit explanation.)

Chapter 12

PAYROLL, NOTES PAYABLE, AND OTHER CURRENT LIABILITIES

STUDY GOALS

After studying this chapter, you should be able to:
1. Prepare the accounting entries for payrolls, including liabilities arising from employee earnings, deductions from earnings, and employer's payroll taxes.
2. List the principal components of accounting systems for payroll and payroll taxes.
3. List the principles of internal control for payroll systems.
4. Prepare accounting entries for employee fringe benefits, including vacation pay and pensions.
5. Prepare the necessary journal entries for transactions involving short-term notes payable.
6. Prepare the necessary journal entries for accounting for product warranties.

GLOSSARY OF KEY TERMS

Discount. The interest deducted from the maturity value of a note.

Discount rate. The rate used in computing the interest to be deducted from the maturity value of a note.

Employee's earnings record. A detailed record of each employee's earnings.

FICA tax. Federal Insurance Contributions Act tax used to finance federal programs for old-age and disability benefits and health insurance for the aged.

Gross pay. The total earnings of an employee for a pay-

roll period.

Net pay. Gross pay less payroll deductions; the amount the employer is obligated to pay the employee.

Payroll. The total amount paid to employees for a certain period.

Payroll register. A multicolumn form used to assemble and summarize payroll data at the end of each payroll period.

Proceeds. The net amount available from discounting a note.

CHAPTER OUTLINE

I. Payroll.
   A. The term payroll refers to a total amount paid to employees for a certain period.
   B. Payroll expenditures are usually significant for a business enterprise for several reasons:
      1. Employees are sensitive to payroll errors or irregularities, and maintaining good employee morale requires that the payroll be paid on a timely, accurate basis.
      2. Payroll expenditures are subject to various federal and state regulations.
      3. The amount of payroll expenditures and related payroll taxes have a significant effect on the net income of most business enterprises.

II. Liability for Payroll.
   A. Salary and wage rates are determined, in general, by agreement between the employer and employees. Enterprises engaged in interstate commerce must follow the requirements of the Fair Labor Standards Act. This act requires a minimum rate of 1½ times the regular rate for all hours worked in excess of 40 hours per week.
   B. The employee earnings for a period are determined by multiplying the base rate by the hours worked plus any overtime hours by 1½ of the base rate.
   C. Many enterprises pay their employees an annual bonus in addition to their regular salary

or wage. The method used in determining the amount of a profit-sharing bonus may be expressed as a certain percentage of the following:

1. Income before deducting the bonus and income taxes.
2. Income after deducting the bonus but before deducting income taxes.
3. Income before deducting the bonus but after deducting income taxes.
4. Net income after deducting both the bonus and income taxes.

III. Deductions from Employee Earnings.
   A. The total earnings of an employee for a payroll period, including bonuses and overtime pay, are often called the gross pay. From this amount is subtracted one or more deductions to arrive at net pay.
   B. Most employers are required by the Federal Insurance Contributions Act (FICA) to withhold a portion of the earnings of each of their employees as a deduction.
   C. Except for certain types of employment, all employers must withhold a portion of the earnings of their employees for payment of the employees' liability for federal income tax.
   D. Other deductions, such as union dues, employee insurance, etc., may be authorized by employees.

IV. Computation of Employee Net Pay.
   A. Gross earnings for a payroll period less the payroll deductions yields the amount to be paid to the employee, which is often called net pay or take-home pay.
   B. Because there is a ceiling on annual earnings subject to FICA tax, when the amount of FICA tax to withhold from an employee is determined for a period, it is necessary to refer to one of the following cumulative amounts:
      1. Employee gross earnings for the year up to, but not including, the current payroll period.
      2. Employee tax withheld for the year up to, but not including, the current payroll period.
   C. There is no ceiling on the amount of earnings subject to withholding for income taxes and hence no need to consider the cumulative earnings.
   D. The computation of some deductions can be generalized in the form of algorithms (or arithmetic formulas).

V. Liability for Employer's Payroll Taxes.
   A. Most employers are subject to federal and state taxes based on the amount of remuneration earned by their employees. Such taxes are an operating expense of the business.
   B. Employers are required to contribute to the Federal Insurance Contributions Act (FICA)

program for each employee. The tax rate and the maximum amount of employee remuneration entering into an employer's tax base are the same as those applicable to employees.
   C. Unemployment insurance provides temporary relief to those who become unemployed as a result of economic forces beyond their control. Employers are subject to federal and state unemployment compensation taxes on the remuneration of employees.
   D. A few states also collect a state unemployment compensation tax from employees based on employee remuneration.

VI. Accounting Systems for Payroll and Payroll Taxes.
   A. Accounting systems for payroll and payroll taxes are concerned with the records and reports associated with the employer-employee relationship.
   B. The major parts common to most payroll systems are the payroll register, payroll checks, and employee's earnings record.
   C. The multicolumn form used in assembling and summarizing the data needed at the end of each payroll period is called the payroll register. A payroll register will normally have columns for the following items:
      1. Total hours worked for both regular and overtime period.
      2. The salary or hourly rate of the employee.
      3. Taxable earnings for unemployment compensation and FICA.
      4. Deductions for FICA, federal income tax, and other deductions.
      5. Total amount of deductions.
      6. The net amount of take-home pay.
      7. The check number of the payroll check issued to the employee.
      8. Distribution columns for the accounts to be debited for the payroll expense.
   D. The payroll register serves as the basis for preparing the journal entries to record the payroll and related payroll tax expenses.
   E. Payment of the liability for payroll and payroll taxes is recorded in the same manner as payment of other liabilities.
   F. It is important to note that the respective payroll taxes levied against employers become liabilities at the time the related remuneration is paid to employees, rather than at the time the liability to the employees is incurred.
   G. One of the principal outputs of most payroll systems is a series of payroll checks at the end of each pay period for distribution to employees.
      1. Most employers with a large number of employees use a special bank account and payroll checks designed specifically for payroll.
      2. Currency may be used as a medium of

payment when payroll is paid each week or when the business location or time of payment is such that banking or check-cashing facilities are not readily available to employees.

H. Detailed records must be maintained for each employee in a record called the employee's earnings record. Such a record maintains data on total hours worked, gross earnings, deductions, and net pay.

VII. Payroll System Diagram.
  A. The flow of data within segments of an accounting system may be shown by diagrams.
  B. Through the use of diagrams, interrelationships of the principal parts of a payroll system may be shown.
    1. The output of the payroll system is the payroll register, the payroll checks, earnings records, and reports for tax and other purposes.
    2. The basic data entering the payroll system are called the input of the system. Input data that remain relatively unchanged are characterized as constants. Those data that differ from period to period are termed variables.

VIII. Internal Controls for Payroll Systems.
  A. The cash disbursement controls discussed in earlier chapters are applicable to payrolls. Thus, the use of the voucher system and the requirement that all payments be supported by vouchers are desirable.
  B. Other controls include proper authorization for additions and deletions of employees and the maintenance of attendance records.

IX. Liability for Employees' Fringe Benefits.
  A. Many companies provide their employees a variety of benefits in addition to salary and wages earned. These benefits are referred to as fringe benefits and include vacation pay and pensions.
  B. To properly match revenue and expense, the employer should accrue the vacation pay liability as the vacation privilege is earned, assuming that the payment is probable and can be reasonably estimated. The entry to accrue vacation pay is to debit Vacation Pay Expense and credit a liability, Vacation Pay Payable.
  C. Most companies maintain retirement pension plans for employees. Such plans may be classified as follows:
    1. A contributory plan requires the employer to withhold a portion of each employee's earnings as a contribution to the plan.
    2. A noncontributory plan requires the employer to bear the entire cost.
    3. A funded plan requires the employer to set aside funds to meet future pension benefits by making payments to an independent funding agency.

4. An unfunded plan is managed entirely by the employer instead of by an independent agency.
    5. A qualified plan is designed to comply with federal income tax requirements which allow the employer to deduct pension contributions for tax purposes and which exempt pension fund income from tax. Most pension plans are qualified.
  D. The recording of pension costs involves a debit to Pension Expense. If the pension cost is fully funded, the credit is to Cash. If the pension cost is partially funded, any unfunded amount is credited to Unfunded Accrued Pension Cost.
  E. When an employer first adopts or changes a pension plan, the employer must consider whether to grant employees credit for prior years service. If credit is granted for past service, a prior service cost obligation must be recognized.

X. Notes Payable and Interest Expense.
  A. Notes may be issued to creditors in temporary satisfaction of an account payable created earlier, or they may be issued at the time merchandise or other assets are purchased. The entries to record a note payable are:
    1. Debit Accounts Payable and credit Notes Payable for the issuance of a note in temporary satisfaction of an account payable.
    2. Debit Cash or other asset and credit Notes Payable for notes initially issued.
  B. Interest must be recognized on notes payable.
    1. An adjusting entry debiting Interest Expense and crediting Interest Payable must normally be made at the end of the year to record the accrual of any interest.
    2. A reversing entry is normally made for all accrued interest after the accounts are closed.
    3. When notes are paid at maturity, the entry is normally to debit Notes Payable, debit Interest Expense, and credit Cash for the maturity amount.
  C. Notes may be issued when money is borrowed from banks. Such notes may be interest-bearing or non-interest-bearing.
    1. An interest-bearing note is recorded by debiting Cash and crediting Notes Payable for the face value of the note. At the due date, Notes Payable is debited for the face value of the note, Interest Expense is debited for the interest, and Cash is credited for the total amount due.
    2. When a non-interest-bearing note is issued to a bank, the entry to record the note is to debit Cash for the proceeds, debit Interest Expense for the difference between the face value of the note and the proceeds re-

ceived, and credit Notes Payable for the amount of the face of the note. If the note is paid at maturity, Notes Payable is debited for the face value and Cash is credited.

XI. Product Warranty Liability.

    A. At the time of sale, a company may grant a warranty on a product. If revenues and expenses are to be matched properly, a liability to cover the warranty must be recorded in the period of the sale.

    B. The entry to accrue warranty liability is to debit Product Warranty Expense and credit Product Warranty Payable.

    C. When a defective product is repaired, the repair costs should be recorded by debiting Product Warranty Payable and crediting Cash, Supplies, or another appropriate account.

Name _____

PART 1

Instructions: A list of terms and related statements appear below. From the list of terms, select the one that relates to each statement and print its identifying letter in the space provided.

A. Discount   **E.** Gross pay   **H.** Proceeds
B. Employee's earnings record   **F.** Noncontributory plan   **I.** Salary
C. FICA tax   **G.** Payroll register   **J.** Wages
D. Funded plan

_____ **1.** Payment for managerial, administrative, or similar services, usually expressed in terms of a month or a year.

_____ **2.** Remuneration for manual labor, computed on an hourly, weekly, or piecework basis.

_____ **3.** The total earnings of an employee for a payroll period.

_____ **4.** Employees' contribution to the combined federal programs for old-age and disability benefits, insurance benefits to survivors, and health insurance for the aged.

_____ **5.** Multicolumn form used in assembling and summarizing the data needed at the end of each payroll period.

_____ **6.** A detailed record of an employee's earnings for each payroll period and for the year.

_____ **7.** A pension plan requiring the employer to bear the entire cost.

_____ **8.** A pension plan requiring the employer to set aside funds to meet future pension benefits by making payments to an independent funding agency.

_____ **9.** The amount of interest deducted from a future value.

_____ **10.** The net amount available to a borrower of funds.

PART 2

Instructions: Indicate whether each of the following statements is true or false by placing a check mark in the appropriate column.

	True	False
1. The total earnings of an employee for a payroll period are called net pay.	_____	_____
2. Employers are required to contribute to the Federal Insurance Contributions Act program for each employee.	_____	_____
3. All states require that unemployment compensation taxes be withheld from employees' pay.	_____	_____
4. The payroll register may be used as a posting medium in a manner similar to that in which the voucher register and the check register are used..	_____	_____
5. The amounts withheld from employees' earnings have no effect on the firm's debits to the salary or wage expense accounts...	_____	_____
6. All payroll taxes levied against employers become liabilities at the time the related remuneration is paid to employees.	_____	_____
7. The recording procedures when special payroll checks are used are different from the procedures when the checks are drawn on the regular bank account.	_____	_____
8. Depending on when it is to be paid, vacation liability may be classified in the balance sheet as either a current liability or a long-term liability..	_____	_____
9. If pension cost is partially funded, the employer's contribution to a pension plan for the pension cost for a given year is recorded by a debit to Pension Expense and credits to Cash and Unfunded Accrued Pension Cost...	_____	_____
10. In order for revenues and expenses to be matched properly, a liability to cover the cost of a product warranty must be recorded in the period when the product is repaired....................	_____	_____

PART 3

Instructions: Complete each of the following statements by circling the letter of the best answer.

1. An employee's rate of pay is $12 per hour, with time and a half for hours worked in excess of 40 during a week. If the employee works 50 hours during a week, and has FICA tax withheld at a rate of 7.5% and federal income tax withheld at a rate of 15%, the employee's net pay for the week is
   a. $465
   b. $511.50
   c. $561
   d. $660

2. For good internal control, the addition or deletion of names on the payroll should be supported by written authorization from the
   a. employee being added or deleted
   b. employee's foreman
   c. personnel department
   d. treasurer

3. Which of the following items would not be considered a fringe benefit?
   a. vacations
   b. employee pension plans
   c. health insurance
   d. FICA benefits

4. For proper matching of revenues and expenses, the estimated cost of fringe benefits must be recognized as an expense of the period during which the
   a. employee earns the benefit
   b. employee is paid the benefit
   c. fringe benefit contract is signed
   d. fringe benefit contract becomes effective

5. A pension plan which complies with federal income tax requirements which allow the employer to deduct contributions for tax purposes and which exempt pension fund income from tax is called a
   a. contributory plan
   b. funded plan
   c. model plan
   d. qualified plan

PART 4

Instructions: In each of the following situations, determine the correct amount.

(1) During the current pay period, an employee earned $1,500. Prior to the current period, the employee earned (in the current year) $44,000. If the FICA tax rate is 7.5% on maximum annual earnings of $45,000, what is the amount to be withheld from the employee's pay this period? $ _____

(2) Using the rate and maximum base as in (1), what is the amount of FICA tax withheld from the pay of an employee who has earned $10,000 but has actually received only $9,600, with the remaining $400 to be paid in the next year? $ _____

(3) An employee of a firm operating under the Wage and Hour Law worked 48 hours last week. If the hourly rate of pay is $12, what is the employee's gross earnings for the week? $ _____

PART 5

The weekly gross payroll of Goodman Co. on January 14 amounts to $40,000. The following amounts are to be withheld: FICA tax, $3,000; employees' income tax, $3,200; union dues, $900; and United Way, $800. The $40,000 payroll is distributed as follows: sales salaries, $29,000, and office salaries, $11,000.

Instructions: Omitting explanations, prepare general journal entries to:
(1) Record the payroll.

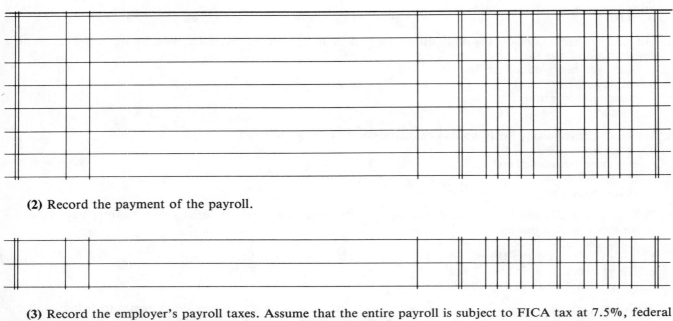

(2) Record the payment of the payroll.

(3) Record the employer's payroll taxes. Assume that the entire payroll is subject to FICA tax at 7.5%, federal unemployment tax at .8%, and state unemployment tax at 2.7%.

Name _____

PART 6

The president of Milton Manufacturing Co. is to be granted an 8% profit-sharing bonus. The corporate income tax rate is 40%. The company's income before the deduction of the income tax and the bonus amounted to $600,000.

Instructions: Calculate the president's bonus under each of the following methods. (Show your work.)

(1) Bonus based on income before deducting either bonus or income tax.

(2) Bonus based on income after deducting bonus but before deducting income tax.

(3) Bonus based on income before deducting bonus but after deducting income tax.

(4) Bonus based on net income after deducting both bonus and income tax.

PART 7

Instructions: For each of the employees listed below, compute the taxes indicated as well as the total of each tax. Assume a 7.5% FICA tax rate on a maximum of $45,000, a state unemployment tax rate of 2.7% on a maximum of $7,000, and a federal unemployment tax rate of .8% on a maximum of $7,000.

Employee	Annual Earnings	Employee's FICA Tax	Employer's Taxes			
			FICA	State Unemployment	Federal Unemployment	Total
Conkle	$ 48,000					
Jacka	$ 6,000					
Kogen	$ 8,000					
Schmid	$ 40,000					
Total	$102,000					

PART 8

Instructions: Prepare the general journal entries to record each of the following items for AT Co. (Omit explanations.)

(1) Accrued employee vacation pay at the end of the year is $6,300.

JOURNAL

PAGE

	DATE	DESCRIPTION	POST. REF.	DEBIT	CREDIT	
1						1
2						2

(2) The estimated product warranty liability at the end of the year is 2% of sales of $140,000.

JOURNAL

PAGE

	DATE	DESCRIPTION	POST. REF.	DEBIT	CREDIT	
1						1
2						2

(3) A partially funded pension plan is maintained for employees, with an annual cost of $41,000. At the end of the year, $27,000 is paid to the fund trustee and the remaining accrued pension liability is recognized.

JOURNAL

PAGE

	DATE	DESCRIPTION	POST. REF.	DEBIT	CREDIT	
1						1
2						2
3						3

PART 9

Instructions: Prepare the general journal entries to record the following transactions. (Omit explanations.)

(1) Audrey Proska borrowed $8,000 from the bank and gave the bank a 90-day, 12% note.

JOURNAL   PAGE

	DATE		DESCRIPTION	POST. REF.	DEBIT	CREDIT	
1							1
2							2

(2) Proska paid the note in (1) at maturity.

JOURNAL   PAGE

	DATE		DESCRIPTION	POST. REF.	DEBIT	CREDIT	
1							1
2							2
3							3

(3) Todd Lesser borrowed $7,000 from the bank, giving a 90-day non-interest-bearing note which was discounted at 12%.

JOURNAL   PAGE

	DATE		DESCRIPTION	POST. REF.	DEBIT	CREDIT	
1							1
2							2
3							3

(4) Lesser paid the note recorded in (3) at maturity.

JOURNAL   PAGE

	DATE		DESCRIPTION	POST. REF.	DEBIT	CREDIT	
1							1
2							2

Page not used

Chapter 13

CONCEPTS AND PRINCIPLES

STUDY GOALS

After studying this chapter, you should be able to:
1. Explain what is meant by the term principle as used in the context of generally accepted accounting principles.
2. List the major organizations which have influenced the establishment of generally accepted accounting principles.
3. List and briefly describe the ten basic accounting concepts and principles.

GLOSSARY OF KEY TERMS

Adequate disclosure. The concept that financial statements and their accompanying footnotes should contain all of the pertinent data believed essential to the reader's understanding of an enterprise's financial status.

American Institute of Certified Public Accountants (AICPA). The national professional organization of CPAs.

Business entity concept. The concept that assumes that accounting applies to individual economic units and that each unit is separate and distinct from the persons who supply its assets.

Completed-contract method. The method that recognizes revenue from long-term construction contracts when the project is completed.

Conservatism. The concept that dictates that in selecting among alternatives, the method or procedure that yields the lesser amount of net income or asset value should be selected.

Consistency. The concept that assumes that the same generally accepted accounting principles have been applied in the preparation of successive financial statements.

Constant dollar. Historical costs that have been converted into dollars of constant value through the use of a price-level index.

Current cost. The amount of cash that would have to be paid currently to acquire assets of the same age and in the same condition as existing assets.

Financial Accounting Standards Board (FASB). The current authoritative body for the development of accounting principles for all entities except state and municipal governments.

Going concern concept. The concept that assumes that a business entity has a reasonable expectation of continuing in business at a profit for an indefinite period of time.

Governmental Accounting Standards Board (GASB). The current authoritative body for the development of accounting principles for state and municipal governments.

Installment method. The method of recognizing revenue, whereby each receipt of cash from installment sales is considered to be composed of partial payment of cost of merchandise sold and gross profit.

Internal Revenue Service (IRS). The branch of the U.S. Treasury Department concerned with enforcement and collection of the income tax.

Matching. The principle of accounting that all revenues should be matched with the expenses incurred in earning those revenues during a period of time.

Materiality. The concept that recognizes the practicality of ignoring small or insignificant deviations from generally accepted accounting principles.

Percentage-of-completion method. The method of recognizing revenue from long-term contracts over the entire life of the contract.

Point of sale method. The method of recognizing revenue, whereby the revenue is determined to be realized at the time that title passes to the buyer.

Price-level index. The ratio of the total cost of a group of commodities prevailing at a particular time to the total cost of the same group of commodities at an earlier base time.

Securities and Exchange Commission (SEC). The federal agency that exercises a dominant influence over the development of accounting principles for most companies whose securities are traded in interstate commerce.

CHAPTER OUTLINE

I. Development of Concepts and Principles.
  A. The word "principle" as used in the context of generally accepted accounting principles does not have the same authoritativeness as universal principles or natural laws. Instead, accounting principles represent the best possible guides, based on reason, observation, and experimentation, to make accounting data more useful in an ever-changing society.
  B. The Financial Accounting Standards Board (FASB) is presently the dominant body in the development of generally accepted accounting principles. The FASB replaced the Accounting Principles Board (APB) in 1973.
    1. After issuing discussion memoranda and preliminary proposals and evaluating comments from interested parties, the FASB issues *Statements of Financial Accounting Standards,* which become part of generally accepted accounting principles.
    2. The FASB also issues *Interpretations* which have the same authority as the standards.
    3. Presently, the FASB is in the process of developing a broad conceptual framework for financial accounting through the issuance of *Statements of Financial Accounting Concepts.* To date, six concepts have been issued.
  C. The Governmental Accounting Standards Board (GASB) was formed in 1984 to establish accounting standards to be followed by state and municipal governments.
  D. Other accounting organizations that are influential in the establishment of accounting principles include the American Institute of Certified Public Accountants (AICPA) and the American Accounting Association (AAA). Each of these organizations publishes a monthly or quarterly periodical and, from time to time, issues other publications in the form of research studies, technical opinions, and monographs.
  E. Various governmental agencies with an interest in the development of accounting principles include the Securities and Exchange Commission (SEC) and the Internal Revenue Service (IRS).
  F. Other influential organizations in the development of accounting principles include the Financial Executives Institute (FEI), the National Association of Accountants (NAA), the Financial Analysts Federation, and the Securities Industry Associates.
II. Business Entity.
  A. The business entity concept assumes that a business enterprise is separate and distinct from the persons who supply its assets, regardless of the legal form of the entity.
  B. The accounting process is primarily concerned with the business entity as a productive economic unit and only secondarily concerned with the investor as a claimant to the assets of the business.
III. Going Concern.
  A. The going concern concept assumes that a business entity has a reasonable expectation of continuing in business at a profit for an indefinite period of time.
  B. The going concern concept provides much of the justification for recording plant assets at acquisition cost and depreciating them in an orderly manner without reference to their current realizable values.
  C. Doubt as to the continued existence of a firm may be disclosed in a note to the financial statements.
  D. When there is conclusive evidence that a business entity has a limited life, the accounting procedures should be appropriate to the expected terminal date of the entity. In such circumstances, the financial statements should be prepared from a "quitting concern" or liquidation point of view, rather than a "going concern" point of view.
IV. Objective Evidence.
  A. In order to maintain the confidence of the many users of the financial statements, entries in the accounting records and the data reported on financial statements must be based on objectively determined evidence.
  B. Evidence may not always be conclusively objective; in such circumstances, the most objective evidence available should be used.
V. Unit of Measurement.
  A. All business transactions are recorded in terms of money. It is only through the record of dollar amounts that the diverse transactions and activities of a business may be measured, reported, and periodically compared.
  B. The scope of accounting reports is generally limited to those factors that can be expressed in monetary terms.
  C. As a unit of measurement, the dollar is characterized by its instability of purchasing power.
    1. The use of a monetary unit that is assumed to be stable insures objectivity. The use of current cost data is one method of supplementing the conventional statements so as to report the effects of changing price levels.
      a. Current cost is the amount of cash that would have to be paid currently to ac-

quire assets of the same age and same condition as existing assets.

    b. The use of current costs permits the identification of gains and losses that result from holding assets during periods of changes in price levels.

    c. The major disadvantage in the use of current costs is the absence of established standards and procedures for determining such costs.

  2. Constant dollar data may also be used for supplementing financial statements so as to report the effects of changing price levels.

    a. A price-level index is the ratio of the total cost of a group of commodities prevailing at a particular time to the total cost of the same group of commodities at an earlier base time.

    b. A general price-level index may be used to determine the effect of changes in price levels on certain financial statement items by computing constant dollar equivalents.

VI. Accounting Period.

  A. A complete and accurate picture of an enterprise's success or failure cannot be obtained until it discontinues operations, converts its assets into cash, and pays off its debts.

  B. Because many decisions must be made by management and interested outsiders throughout the life of a business entity, periodic reports on operations, financial position, and changes in financial position are prepared.

VII. Matching Revenue and Expired Costs.

  A. The determination of periodic net income is a two-fold problem involving the revenue recognized during the period, and the matching of expired costs against that revenue.

  B. Various criteria exist for determining when it is acceptable to recognize revenue for merchandise delivered or services rendered to customers.

    1. Revenue from the sale of merchandise is usually determined by the point of sale method, under which revenue is realized at the time title passes to the buyer.

    2. The recognition of revenue may be delayed until payment is received. When this criterion is used, revenue is considered to be realized at the time the cash is collected, regardless of when the sale was made. This method has the practical advantage of simplicity, and may be used by professional services enterprises.

    3. Under the installment method of determining revenue (used primarily in the retail field), each receipt of cash is considered to be revenue and to be composed of partial amounts of the cost of merchandise sold and gross profit on the sale.

    4. Under the percentage-of-completion method, the revenue to be recognized and the income for a year are determined by the estimated percentage of the contract that has been completed during the period. This estimated percentage can be developed by comparing the incurred costs with the most recent estimates of total costs or by estimates by engineers, architects, or other qualified personnel of the progress of the work performed.

    5. In general, there are two approaches to allocating costs to be matched against revenues.

      a. Cost allocations may be determined by computing the amount of expired costs.

      b. Cost allocations may be determined by computing the amount of unexpired costs.

  C. Many of the costs allocable to a period are treated as an expense at the time of incurrence because they will be wholly expired at the end of the period. For example, when a monthly rent is paid at the beginning of a month, the cost incurred is unexpired and hence is an asset; but since the cost incurred will be wholly expired at the end of the month, the rental is usually charged directly to the appropriate expense account.

VIII. Adequate Disclosure.

  A. Under the adequate disclosure concept, financial statements and their accompanying footnotes or other explanatory materials should contain all the pertinent data believed essential to the reader's understanding of the enterprise's financial status.

  B. When there are several acceptable alternative accounting methods that could have a significant effect on amounts reported on the statements, the particular method used should be disclosed.

  C. In situations where an accounting estimate has been changed or otherwise revised, the effect of the change or revision on net income should be disclosed in the financial statements for the year of the change or revision.

  D. Contingent liabilities are potential obligations that will materialize only if certain events occur in the future.

    1. If the amount of the contingent liability is probable and can be reasonably estimated, it should be recorded in the accounts.

    2. If the amount of the contingent liability cannot be reasonably estimated, the details of the contingency should be disclosed.

E. To help financial statement users in assessing past performance and future potential of diversified companies, financial statements should disclose information on the segments of a business, such as the amounts of business in different industries, its foreign markets, and its major customers.

F. Significant events occuring after the close of the period should be disclosed.

IX. Consistency.

A. The concept of consistency does not completely prohibit changes in accounting principles used. However, changes in accounting principles should be fully disclosed in the financial statements.

B. Different accounting methods may be used throughout an enterprise, such as the use of different depreciation methods for different classes of assets or different inventory methods for different classes of inventory.

X. Materiality.

A. The concept of materiality refers to the relative importance of an event, accounting procedure, or change in procedure that affects items on the financial statements.

B. To determine materiality, the size of an item and its nature must be considered in relationship to the size and the nature of other items.

C. The concept of materiality may also be applied to procedures used in recording transactions. For example, small expenditures for plant assets may be treated as an expense of the period rather than as an asset.

XI. Conservatism.

A. Historically, accountants have tended to be conservative, and in selecting among alternatives they have often favored the method or procedure that yields the lesser amount of net income or asset value. This attitude of conservatism was often expressed in a statement to "anticipate no profits and provide for all losses."

B. Current accounting thought has shifted somewhat and conservatism is no longer considered to be a dominant factor in selecting among alternatives.

PART 1

Instructions: A list of terms and related statements appear below. From the list of terms, select the one that relates to each statement and print its identifying letter in the space provided.

A. Business entity concept
B. Conservatism
C. Consistency concept
D. Current cost data

E. General price-level data
F. Going concern concept
G. Installment method
H. Materiality concept

I. Percentage-of-completion method
J. Point of sale method

_____ 1. The concept that assumes that a business enterprise is separate and distinct from the persons who supply its assets.

_____ 2. The concept that assumes that a business entity has a reasonable expectation of continuing in business at a profit for an indefinite period of time.

_____ 3. Data indicating the amount of cash that would have to be paid currently to acquire assets of the same age and in the same condition as existing assets.

_____ 4. Data indicating historical cost amounts that have been converted to constant dollars.

_____ 5. A method under which revenue is realized at the time title passes to the buyer.

_____ 6. A method under which each receipt of cash is considered to be revenue and to be composed of partial amounts of (1) the cost of merchandise sold and (2) gross profit on the sale.

_____ 7. A method under which revenue is realized over the entire life of a long-term contract.

_____ 8. The concept that enables financial statement users to assume that successive financial statements of an enterprise are based on the same generally accepted accounting principles.

_____ 9. The concept that permits accountants to treat small expenditures for plant assets as an expense rather than an asset.

_____ 10. The attitude that leads accountants to prefer the method or procedure that yields the lesser amount of net income or of asset value.

PART 2

Instructions: Indicate whether each of the following statements is true or false by placing a check mark in the appropriate column.

	True	False
1. There is likely to be less differentiation between "management" and "outsiders" in a business enterprise as it increases in size and complexity..	____	____
2. The "principles" used in accounting are similar to the natural laws relating to the physical sciences	____	____
3. General acceptance among the members of the accounting profession is the criterion for determining an accounting principle	____	____
4. Responsibility for the development of accounting principles has rested primarily with the federal government	____	____
5. The FASB replaced the Accounting Principles Board	____	____
6. The FASB Statements of Financial Accounting Concepts are intended to provide a broad conceptual framework for accounting	____	____
7. The GASB has responsibility for establishing the accounting standards to be followed by state and municipal governments	____	____
8. The SEC is a branch of the FASB	____	____
9. The business entity concept used in accounting for a sole proprietorship is the same as the legal concept of a sole proprietorship	____	____
10. The going concern assumption supports the treatment of virtually unsalable prepaid expenses as assets	____	____
11. In a going concern, plant assets usually are recorded on the balance sheet at their estimated realizable values	____	____
12. According to the objective evidence principle, entries in the accounting records and data reported on financial statements must be based on objectively determined evidence	____	____
13. The major disadvantage in the use of current costs is the absence of established standards and procedures for determining such costs..	____	____
14. Large, publicly held companies are required to disclose both current cost and constant dollar information annually as supplemental data	____	____
15. A complete and accurate picture of an enterprise's success or failure cannot be obtained until it discontinues operations, converts its assets into cash, and pays off its debts	____	____
16. In recent years, financial statement emphasis has shifted from the income statement to the balance sheet...	____	____
17. Revenue from the sale of goods generally is considered to be realized at the time title passes to the buyer	____	____
18. Revenue considered to be earned at the time the cash is collected, regardless of when the sale was made, is recorded on the cash basis	____	____
19. The percentage-of-completion method permits revenue to be recognized based on an estimate of the percentage of a contract that has been completed during a period.........................	____	____
20. The percentage-of-completion method usually is more objective than the point of sale method ..	____	____
21. The amount of cash or equivalent given to acquire property or service is referred to as its cost ...	____	____
22. As assets are sold or used, they become "expired costs" or liabilities	____	____

23. Criteria for standards of disclosure must be based on objective facts rather than on value judgements ....   _____   _____

24. When there are several acceptable alternative accounting methods that could have a significant effect on amounts reported on the statements, the particular method used should be disclosed ..   _____   _____

25. It is acceptable to revise accounting estimates based on additional information or subsequent developments ....   _____   _____

26. If a contingent liability is probable and the amount of the liability can be reasonably estimated, it should be recorded in the accounts ....   _____   _____

27. The concept of consistency prohibits changes in accounting principles employed ....   _____   _____

28. The consistency concept requires that a specific accounting method be applied uniformly throughout an enterprise...   _____   _____

PART 3

Instructions: Complete each of the following statements by circling the letter of the best answer.

1. At the present time, the dominant body in the development of generally accepted accounting principles is the
   a. AICPA
   b. FASB
   c. APB
   d. GASB

2. The statements of generally accepted accounting principles issued by the FASB are called
   a. Statements of Accounting Principles
   b. Statements of FAF
   c. Statements of Financial Accounting Standards
   d. FASB Opinions

3. Of the various governmental agencies with an interest in the development of accounting principles, the one that has been the most influential has been the
   a. SEC
   b. IRS
   c. GASB
   d. FEI

4. The organization of accountants that is primarily concerned with management's use of accounting information in directing business operations is the
   a. FEI
   b. AAA
   c. AICPA
   d. NAA

5. For a number of reasons, including custom and various legal requirements, the maximum interval between accounting reports is
   a. one month
   b. three months
   c. one year
   d. three years

6. When circumstances are such that the collection of receivables is not reasonably assured, a method that may be used to determine revenue is called the
   a. installment method
   b. post-sale method
   c. gross profit method
   d. point of sale method

7. If property other than cash is given to acquire property, the cost of the acquired property is considered to be the
   a. net realizable value of the acquired property
   b. current cost of the property given
   c. list price of the acquired property
   d. cash equivalent of the property given

8. If an enterprise suffers a major loss from a fire between the end of the year and the issuance of the financial statements, the enterprise should
   a. not mention the loss in the statements because it occurred in a different accounting period
   b. disclose the loss in a note to the statements
   c. not mention the loss in the statements, but put out a separate announcement of the loss
   d. record the loss in the accounting records and in the statements

9. For each significant reporting segment of a business, an enterprise is required to disclose each of the following except
   a. revenue
   b. income from operations
   c. identifiable assets associated with the segment
   d. identifiable liabilities associated with the segment

10. Of the following accounting concepts, the least important one in choosing among alternative accounting methods is
    a. conservatism
    b. objectivity
    c. consistency
    d. materiality

PART 4

Instructions: In each of the following situations, determine the correct amounts.

(1) Fifteen years ago, Felix Corporation bought a building for $250,000. The company has taken depreciation of $10,000 a year on this building. Recently, the building was appraised at $125,000. Another firm offered to buy the building for $130,000. Felix Corporation should report this building on its balance sheet at the amount of .... $ _____

(2) On January 1, Nancy Company paid $8,400 for a 3-year insurance policy. The company should report insurance expense for the second year in the amount of .... $ _____

(3) Perez Company was organized on January 1. All sales are made on the installment plan and gross profits are calculated by the installment method. During the first year, sales amounted to $1,890,000; cost of sales, $1,323,000; and collections, $980,000. The gross profit for the first year was .... $ _____

(4) Yellow Sales Company, organized January 1, makes all sales on the installment plan but calculates gross profits by using the point of sale method. During the first year, the company's sales amounted to $1,890,000; cost of sales, $1,323,000; and collections on installments, $980,000. The gross profit for the year was .... $ _____

(5) Eunice Quick established a sole proprietorship business. During the first month, she wrote checks for $15,000 on the business bank account. Of this amount, she spent $7,000 for personal needs and $8,000 for merchandise for the business. The net worth of the business was decreased by .... $ _____

PART 5

During the current year, Salem Construction Company contracted to build a new basketball arena for the local university. The total contract price was $6,800,000 and the estimated construction costs were $5,250,000. At the end of the current year, the project was estimated to be 30% completed and the costs incurred totaled $1,430,000.

Instructions: Using the percentage-of-completion method of recognizing revenue, determine the following amounts:

(1) Revenue from the contract .... $ _____

(2) Cost associated with the contract .... $ _____

(3) Income from the contract recognized for the current year .... $ _____

PART 6

Foolum Co.'s net income for its first year of operations is $60,900, based on fifo inventory and straight-line depreciation. Foolum is considering making two accounting changes in the current year, as follows:
  (1) From fifo to lifo inventory. Fifo inventory cost is $17,000, whereas lifo inventory cost would be $14,100.
  (2) From straight-line to declining-balance depreciation at twice the straight-line rate. Straight-line depreciation is $8,300, whereas declining-balance depreciation would be $11,700.

Instructions: In the spaces provided below, compute the net income if the two accounting changes are made.

Net income using fifo and straight-line $60,900

(1) Effect of inventory change .... $ _____

(2) Effect of depreciation change .... $ _____

(3) Revised net income .... $ _____

PART 7

Closenuf Co. reported net income for the current year of $33,000. In reviewing Closenuf's records, you discover the following items for which no adjustments were made at the end of the period.

(1) Supplies of $23 were on hand.
(2) Interest expense of $12 had accrued for 4 days on a note payable.
(3) Delivery charges of $16 on packages received in the current period were not entered until paid in the following period.
(4) Petty cash expenditures of $5 were not entered because reimbursement of petty cash was not made at the end of the period.

Instructions: (1) In the space provided below, compute the net income of Closenuf Co. for the year if adjustments were made for these items.

Reported net income $33,000

a. Supplies . . . . $ _____

b. Interest expense . . . . $ _____

c. Delivery charges . . . . $ _____

d. Petty cash expenditures . . . . $ _____

e. Revised net income . . . . $ _____

(2) What accounting concept would support Closenuf's not making these adjustments?

Chapter 14

PARTNERSHIP FORMATION, INCOME DIVISION, AND LIQUIDATION

STUDY GOALS

After studying this chapter, you should be able to:

1. List the basic characteristics of partnership organization and operations which have accounting implications.

2. Prepare journal entries for the formation of a partnership.

3. Prepare journal entries for the admission of a new partner to an existing partnership.

4. Prepare journal entries for the withdrawal of partners.

5. Prepare journal entries for the liquidation of a partnership.

6. Prepare financial statements for a partnership.

GLOSSARY OF KEY TERMS

Articles of partnership. The formal written contract creating a partnership.

Deficiency. The debit balance in the retained earnings account.

Liquidation. The winding-up process when a partnership goes out of business.

Realization. The sale of assets when a partnership is being liquidated.

CHAPTER OUTLINE

I. Characteristics of Partnerships.
   A. The Uniform Partnership Act defines a partnership as "an association of two or more persons to carry on as co-owners a business for profit."
   B. Partnerships have several characteristics that have accounting implications.
      1. A partnership has a limited life. Dissolution of a partnership occurs whenever a partner ceases to be a member of the firm for any reason.
      2. Most partnerships are general partnerships, in which the partners have unlimited liability. Each partner is individually liable to creditors for debts incurred by the partnership.
      3. In some states, a limited partnership may be formed, in which the liability of some partners may be limited to the amount of their capital investment. However, a limited partnership must have at least one general partner who has unlimited liability.

   4. Partners have co-ownership of partnership property. The property invested in a partnership by a partner becomes the property of all the partners jointly.
   5. The mutual agency characteristic of a partnership means that each partner is an agent of the partnership, with the authority to enter into contracts for the partnership. Thus, the acts of each partner bind the partnership and become the responsibility of all partners.
   6. A significant right of partners is participation in income of the partnership. Net income and net loss are distributed among the partners according to their agreement. In the absence of any agreement, all partners share equally.
   7. Although partnerships are nontaxable entities and therefore do not pay federal income taxes, they must file an information return with the Internal Revenue Service.
   C. A partnership is created by a voluntary contract containing all the elements essential to

any other enforceable contract. This contract is known as the articles of partnership or partnership agreement.

II. Advantages and Disadvantages of Partnerships.
  A. Advantages of a partnership form of organization include the following:
    1. A partnership is relatively easy and inexpensive to organize, requiring only an agreement between two or more persons.
    2. A partnership has the advantage of being able to bring together more capital, more managerial skills, and more experience than a sole proprietorship.
    3. A partnership is a nontaxable entity; the combined income taxes paid by the individual partners may be lower than the income taxes that would be paid by a corporation.
  B. The disadvantages of a partnership form of organization are as follows:
    1. The partnership life is limited.
    2. Each partner has unlimited liability and one partner can bind the partnership to contracts.
    3. Raising large amounts of capital is more difficult for a partnership than for a corporation.

III. Accounting for Partnerships.
  A. Most of the day-to-day accounting for a partnership is the same as the accounting for any other form of business organization.
  B. Differences in accounting arise primarily in the areas of formation, income distribution, dissolution, and liquidation of partnerships.

IV. Recording Investments.
  A. A separate entry is made for the investment of each partner in a partnership.
    1. The various assets contributed by a partner are debited to the proper asset accounts.
    2. If liabilities are assumed by the partnership, the appropriate liability accounts are credited.
    3. The partner's capital account is credited for the net amount.
  B. The monetary amounts at which noncash assets are recorded by a partnership are those agreed upon by the partners. In arriving at an appropriate amount for such assets, consideration should be given to their market values at the time the partnership is formed.
  C. Receivables contributed to the partnership are recorded at their face amount, with a credit to a contra account if provision is to be made for possible future uncollectibility.

V. Division of Net Income or Net Loss.
  A. Distribution and division of income or loss among partners should be in conformity with the partnership agreement. As indicated previously, if the partnership agreement is silent on the matter, the law provides that all partners should share equally.
  B. As a means of recognizing diferences in ability and in amount of time devoted to the business, articles of partnership often provide for the division of a portion of net income to the partners in the form of a salary allowance.
    1. The articles may also provide for withdrawals of cash by the partners in lieu of salary payments.
    2. A clear distinction must therefore be made between the division of net income, which is credited to the capital accounts, and payments to the partners, which are debited to the drawing accounts.
  C. Partners may agree that the most equitable plan of income sharing is to allow salaries based on the services rendered and also to allow interest on their capital investments.
  D. If the net income is less than the total of the special allowances (salaries and interest), the "remaining balance" to be distributed will be a negative figure that must be divided among the partners as though it were a net loss.

VI. Statements for Partnerships.
  A. Details of the division of net income should be disclosed in the financial statements prepared at the end of the fiscal period.
  B. Details of the changes in the owner's equity of a partnership during the period should also be presented in a statement of owner's equity.

VII. Partnership Dissolution.
  A. Because one of the basic characteristics of the partnership form of organization is its limited life, any change in the personnel of the ownership results in the dissolution of the partnership.
    1. Admission of a new partner dissolves the old partnership.
    2. Death, bankruptcy, or withdrawal of a partner causes dissolution of the partnership.
  B. Dissolution of the partnership is not necessarily followed by the winding up of the affairs of the business. In many cases, the remaining partners may continue to operate the business. When this happens, a new partnership is formed and new articles of partnership are prepared.
  C. An additional person may be admitted to a partnership enterprise only with the consent of all the current partners.
  D. An additional partner may be admitted to a partnership through either of two procedures:
    1. A new partner may be admitted with the purchase of an interest from one or more of the current partners. In this case, neither the total assets nor the total

owner's equity of the business is affected. The purchase price of the partnership share is paid directly to the selling partner or partners. The only accounting entry needed is to transfer the proper amounts of owner's equity from the capital accounts of the selling partner or partners to the capital account established for the incoming partner.

2. A new partner may be admitted to the partnership through the contribution of assets directly to the partnership. In this case, both the total assets and the total owner's equity of the business are increased. The assets contributed to the partnership are debited and the capital account of the incoming partner is credited.

3. Whenever a new partner is admitted to a partnership, the existing assets of the partnership should be adjusted to their fair market values. The net amount of the increases and decreases in asset values are then allocated to the capital accounts of the old partners according to their income-sharing ratio. It is important that the assets be stated in terms of current prices at the time of admission of the new partner. Failure to recognize current prices may result in the new partner participating in gains or losses attributable to the period prior to admission.

4. When a new partner is admitted to a partnership, goodwill attributable either to the old partnership or to the incoming partner may be recognized. The amount of goodwill agreed upon is recorded as an asset, with a corresponding credit to the appropriate capital accounts.

E. When a partner retires or for some other reason wishes to withdraw from the firm, one or more of the remaining partners may purchase the withdrawing partner's interest and the business may be continued without apparent interruption.

1. The settlement of the purchase and sale is made between the partners as individuals, in a manner similar to the admission of a new partner by purchase of interest, and thus is not recorded by the partnership.

2. The only entry required by the partnership is a debit to the capital account of the partner withdrawing and a credit to the capital account of the partner or partners acquiring the interest.

F. When a partner retires or for some other reason wishes to withdraw from the firm, the settlement with the withdrawing partner may be made by the partnership.

1. The effect of this withdrawal is to reduce the assets and the owner's equity of the firm.

2. To determine the ownership equity of the withdrawing partner, the asset accounts should be adjusted to current market prices. The net amount of the adjustment should be divided among the capital accounts of the partners according to the income-sharing ratio.

3. In the event that the cash or the other available assets are insufficient to make complete payment at the time of withdrawal, a liability should be credited for the balance owed to the withdrawing partner.

G. The death of a partner dissolves the partnership and in the absence of any contrary agreement, the accounts should be closed as of the date of death, and the net income for the fractional part of the year should be transferred to the capital accounts.

1. It is not unusual for the partnership agreement to stipulate that the accounts remain open to the end of the fiscal year or until the affairs are wound up, if that should occur earlier.

2. The net income of the entire period is then divided, as provided by the agreement, between the respective periods occurring before and after dissolution.

3. The balance in the capital account of the deceased partner is transferred to a liability account with the deceased's estate. The procedures for settling with the estate will conform to those outlined earlier for the withdrawal of a partner from the business.

VIII. Liquidation of a Partnership.

A. When a partnership goes out of business, it usually sells the assets, pays the creditors, and distributes the remaining cash or other assets to the partners according to their claims. This winding-up process is called liquidation.

B. During the process of liquidation, the sale of assets is called realization. As cash is realized, it is applied first to the payment of the claims of creditors.

C. Any gains or losses realized from the sale of assets should be distributed to the capital accounts of the partners in their income-sharing ratios.

D. After all liabilities have been paid, the remaining cash should be distributed to the partners according to the balances in their capital accounts. Under no circumstances should the income-sharing ratio be used as a basis for distributing cash to the partners after payment of liabilities.

E. The share of a loss from the realization of assets to a partner may exceed the partner's ownership equity (capital account balance). The resulting debit balance in the capital account is called a deficiency.

1. Pending collection from the deficient partner, the partnership cash will not be sufficient to pay the other partners in full.

2. In such cases, the available cash should be distributed in such a manner that, if the claim against the deficient partner cannot be collected, each of the remaining capital balances will be sufficient to absorb the appropriate share of the deficiency.

3. The affairs of the partnership are not completely wound up until the claims against the partners are settled. Payments to the firm by the deficient partner are credited to that partner's capital account. Any cash thus collected is distributed to the remaining partners.

4. Any uncollectible deficiency from a partner becomes a loss to the partnership and is written off against the capital accounts of the remaining partners according to their income-sharing ratios.

F. It should be noted that the type of error most likely to occur in the liquidation of a partnership is an improper distribution of cash to the partners. Errors of this type result from confusing the distribution of cash with the division of gains and losses on realization.

1. Gains and losses on realization result from the disposal of assets to outsiders. These gains and losses should be divided among the capital accounts in the same manner as net income or net loss from ordinary business operations, namely, in the income-sharing ratio.

2. The distribution of cash (or other assets) to the partners upon liquidation is the exact reverse of the contribution of assets by the partners at the time the partnership was established. The distribution of assets to the partnership is equal to the credit balances of the respective capital accounts after all gains and losses on realization have been divided and a proper allowance has been made for any potential partner deficiencies.

PART 1

Instructions: A list of terms and related statements appear below. From the list of terms, select the one that relates to each statement and print its identifying letter in the space provided.

A. Articles of partnership   **E.** Limited life   **I.** Realization
B. Deficiency   **F.** Limited partnership   **J.** Statement of owner's equity
C. General partnership   **G.** Liquidation
D. Income statement   **H.** Mutual agency

_____ 1. A type of partnership in which the partners have unlimited liability.

_____ 2. A type of partnership in which the liability of some partners may be restricted to the amount of their capital investment.

_____ 3. A characteristic of a partnership that means that each partner has the authority to enter into contracts for the partnership.

_____ 4. Another name for the partnership agreement or contract among the partners.

_____ 5. A disadvantage of a partnership.

_____ 6. A statement in which the details of the division of partnership net income may be disclosed.

_____ 7. A statement in which the details of the changes in the owner's equity of a partnership during the period would be presented.

_____ 8. The winding-up process of a partnership may generally be called (?)

_____ 9. When a partnership is going out of business, the sale of the assets is called (?)

_____ 10. When a partnership is going out of business and the loss chargeable to a partner exceeds that partner's ownership equity, the resulting debit balance in the capital account is called a(n) (?)

PART 2

Instructions: Indicate whether each of the following statements is true or false by placing a check mark in the appropriate column.

	True	False
1. When a partner ceases to be a member of the firm for any reason, dissolution of the partnership occurs.	___	___
2. Each general partner is individually liable to creditors for debts incurred by the partnership.	___	___
3. A limited partnership must have at least one general partner who has unlimited liability.	___	___
4. The property invested in a partnership by a partner remains identified as that partner's property.	___	___
5. A partner's claim against the assets of the partnership in the event of dissolution is measured by the amount of the partner's initial investment.	___	___
6. A written contract is necessary to the legal formation of a partnership.	___	___
7. At the time a partnership is formed, the market values of the assets should be considered in determining each partner's investment.	___	___
8. In the absence of an agreement for income or loss distributions among the partners, the partners should share income equally, even if there are differences in their capital contributions.	___	___
9. Regardless of whether partners' salaries and interest are treated as expenses of the partnership or as a division of net income, the total amount allocated to each partner will not be affected.	___	___
10. A partnership is required to pay federal income taxes.	___	___
11. Any change in the personnel of the ownership results in a dissolution of a partnership.	___	___
12. A new partner may be admitted to a partnership with the consent of the majority of the old partners.	___	___
13. A partner's interest may be disposed of only with the consent of the remaining partners.	___	___
14. When a new partner is admitted by purchasing an interest from one or more of the old partners, the purchase price is recorded in the accounts of the partnership.	___	___
15. It is appropriate to adjust the old partnership assets to current market values at the time a new partner is admitted.	___	___
16. At the time a new partner is admitted, goodwill attributable to the incoming partner may be recognized.	___	___
17. When one of the remaining partners purchases a withdrawing partner's interest in the partnership, the only entry required by the partnership is to increase the capital account of the remaining partner by the amount paid to the withdrawing partner.	___	___
18. As cash is realized from the sale of assets during the liquidation of a partnership, the cash is applied first to the payment of the claims of the limited partners.	___	___
19. If the distribution of the loss on the sale of noncash assets when a partnership goes out of business causes a partner's account to have a debit balance, this balance represents a claim of the partnership against the partner.	___	___
20. If a deficiency of a partner is uncollectible, this represents a loss which is written off against the capital balances of the remaining partners.	___	___

PART 3

Instructions: Complete each of the following statements by circling the letter of the best answer.

1. If the partnership agreement specifies that profits should be shared in a 3:2 ratio between two partners but is silent as to losses, losses should be
   a. shared in the ratio of the capital balances
   b. shared in a 3:2 ratio
   c. shared in a 2:3 ratio
   d. shared in the ratio of the capital contributions

2. Which of the following is not an advantage of a partnership?
   a. It is possible to bring together more capital than in a sole proprietorship
   b. Partners' income taxes may be less than the income taxes would be on a corporation
   c. It is possible to bring together more managerial skills than in a sole proprietorship
   d. Each partner has limited liability

3. When a new partner is admitted to the partnership by a contribution of assets to the partnership
   a. neither the total assets nor the total owner's equity of the business is affected
   b. only the total assets are affected
   c. only the owner's equity is affected
   d. both the total assets and the total owner's equity are increased

4. When a partner retires and the settlement with the partner is made by the partnership, the effect is to
   a. reduce the assets and the owner's equity of the firm
   b. reduce the assets and increase the owner's equity of the firm
   c. increase the liabilities and the owner's equity of the firm
   d. leave the assets and owner's equity unchanged

5. If there is a loss on the sale of noncash assets when a partnership goes out of business, the loss should be divided among the partners
   a. according to their original capital investments
   b. according to their current capital balances
   c. according to their income-sharing ratio
   d. equally

PART 4

R. P. Clemens and D. J. Sullivan formed a partnership. Clemens invested $430,000 cash and merchandise valued at $60,000. Sullivan invested $135,000 cash, land valued at $270,000, equipment valued at $60,000, and merchandise valued at $45,000.

Instructions: Prepare the entries to record the investment of Clemens and Sullivan on the partnership books. Use the current date.

JOURNAL

PAGE

	DATE	DESCRIPTION	POST. REF.	DEBIT	CREDIT	
1						1
2						2
3						3
4						4
5						5
6						6
7						7
8						8
9						9

PART 5

On January 2 of the current year, Farris and Shannon formed a partnership in which Farris invested $400,000 and Shannon invested $800,000. During the year, the partnership had a net income of $120,000.

Instructions: Show how this net income would be distributed under each of the following conditions:

(1) The partnership agreement says nothing about the distribution of net income.

Farris' share .... $_____

Shannon's share .... _____

Total .... $_____

(2) The partnership agreement provides that Farris and Shannon are to share net income in a 2:3 ratio respectively.

Farris' share .... $_____

Shannon's share .... _____

Total .... $_____

(3) The partnership agreement provides that Farris and Shannon are to share net income in accordance with the ratio of their original capital investments.

Farris' share .... $_____

Shannon's share .... _____

Total .... $_____

(4) The partnership agreement provides that Farris is to be allowed a salary of $45,000 and Shannon a salary of $25,000, with the balance of net income distributed equally.

DIVISION OF NET INCOME	Farris	Shannon	Total
Salary allowance	$	$	$
Remaining income			
Net income..............	$	$	$120,000

(5) The partnership agreement provides that interest at 5% is to be allowed on the beginning capital and that the balance is to be distributed equally.

DIVISION OF NET INCOME	Farris	Shannon	Total
Interest allowance	$	$	$
Remaining income			
Net income..............	$	$	$120,000

(6) The partnership agreement provides that Farris is to be allowed a salary of $12,000 and Shannon a salary of $18,000; that interest at 5% is to be allowed on beginning capital; and that the balance is to be distributed equally.

DIVISION OF NET INCOME	Farris	Shannon	Total
Salary allowance	$	$	$
Interest allowance			
Remaining income			
Net income	$	$	$120,000

(7) The partnership agreement provides that Farris is to be allowed a salary of $35,000 and Shannon a salary of $37,000; that interest at 5% is to be allowed on beginning capital; and that the balance is to be distributed equally.

DIVISION OF NET INCOME	Farris	Shannon	Total
Salary allowance	$	$	$
Interest allowance			
Total			
Excess of allowances over income			
Net income	$	$	$120,000

PART 6

Ruth Vernon, Joe Parrott, and Gary Forrest are partners having capitals of $125,000, $75,000, and $25,000 respectively. They share net income equally.

Instructions: Prepare the entries (without explanation) to record each of the following situations.

(1) On June 30, Douglas Keith is admitted to the partnership by purchasing one fifth of the respective capital interests of the three partners. He pays $50,000 to Vernon, $35,000 to Parrott, and $25,000 to Forrest.

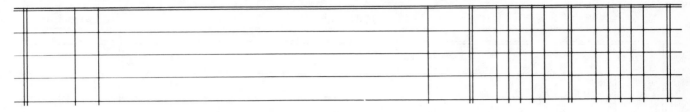

(2) On July 1, Laura Baker is admitted to the partnership for an investment of $65,000, and the parties agree to recognize $30,000 of goodwill attributable to Baker.

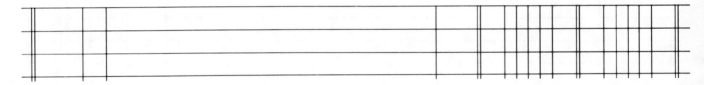

PART 7

Abbott, Bowling, and Cruz are partners having capital balances of $75,000, $65,000, and $60,000 respectively. The partners share net income equally. Cruz has decided to leave the partnership.

Instructions: Prepare the entries (without explanation) to record each of the following independent situations.

(1) The partners agree that the inventory of the partnership should be increased by $12,000 to recognize its fair market value. Abbott buys Cruz's interest in the partnership for $72,000.

JOURNAL

PAGE

DATE	DESCRIPTION	POST. REF.	DEBIT	CREDIT

(2) The partners agree that the inventory of the partnership should be increased by $9,000 to recognize its fair market value. The partnership pays Cruz cash for his interest as reflected by the balance in his capital account.

JOURNAL

PAGE

DATE	DESCRIPTION	POST. REF.	DEBIT	CREDIT

Name _____

PART 8

Prior to the liquidation of the partnership of Tinker, Evers, and Chance, the ledger contained the following accounts and balances: Cash, $100,000; Noncash Assets, $200,000; Liabilities, $60,000; Tinker, Capital, $80,000; Evers, Capital, $50,000; and Chance, Capital, $110,000. Assume that the noncash assets are sold for $270,000. Tinker, Evers, and Chance share profits in a 30:50:20 ratio.

Instructions: (1) Complete the following statement of partnership liquidation, showing the sale of the assets, payment of the liabilities, and the distribution of the remaining cash to the partners.

	Cash +	Noncash Assets =	Liabilities +	Capital Tinker 30% +	Evers 50% +	Chance 20%
Balances before realization	$100,000	$200,000	$60,000	$80,000	$50,000	$110,000
Sale of noncash assets and division of gain						
Balances after realization						
Payment of liabilities						
Balances						
Distribution of cash to partners ..						
Balances						

(2) Assume that the noncash assets are sold for $40,000 and that the partner with a debit balance is unable to pay any part of the deficiency. Complete the following statement of partnership liquidation, showing the sale of the assets, payment of the liabilities, and the distribution of the remaining cash to the partners.

	Cash +	Noncash Assets =	Liabilities +	Capital Tinker 30% +	Evers 50% +	Chance 20%
Balances before realization	$100,000	$200,000	$60,000	$80,000	$50,000	$110,000
Sale of noncash assets and division of loss						
Balances after realization						
Payment of liabilities						
Balances						
Division of deficiency						
Balances						
Distribution of cash to partners ..						
Final balances						

(3) Prepare the journal entries (without explanation) to record the liquidation of the partnership based on the facts in (2). Use the current date.

SOLUTIONS

CHAPTER 1

PART 1

1. F	**4.** J	**7.** A	**10.** B	**13.** I
2. D	**5.** L	**8.** M	**11.** H	**14.** O
3. G	**6.** C	**9.** N	**12.** E	**15.** K

PART 2

1. T	**2.** F	**3.** F	**4.** T	**5.** F
6. T	**7.** F	**8.** T	**9.** F	**10.** T

PART 3

1. d	**2.** c	**3.** b	**4.** d	**5.** a

PART 4

	A	L	OE
1.	+	0	+
2.	+	+	0
3.	+	0	+
4.	+	0	+
5.	−	0	−
6.	+ −	0	0
7.	+ −	0	0
8.	−	−	0
9.	−	−	0
10.	−	0	−

PART 5

	Cash	+	Supplies	+	Land	=	Accts. Pay.	+	Ted Brown, Capital
			Assets			**=**	**Liabilities**	**+**	**Owner's Equity**
1.	$24,000								$24,000I
2.			$2,400				$2,400		
Bal.	$24,000		$2,400				$2,400		$24,000
3.	−12,000				$12,000				
Bal.	$12,000		$2,400		$12,000		$2,400		$24,000
4.	−800						−800		
Bal.	$11,200		$2,400		$12,000		$1,600		$24,000
5.	−1,500								−1,500D
Bal.	$ 9,700		$2,400		$12,000		$1,600		$22,500
6.	−2,000								−2,000E
Bal.	$ 7,700		$2,400		$12,000		$1,600		$20,500
7.							+600		−600E
Bal.	$ 7,700		$2,400		$12,000		$2,200		$19,900
8.	+24,000								+24,000I
Bal.	$31,700		$2,400		$12,000		$2,200		$43,900
9.	+140								+140R
Bal.	$31,840		$2,400		$12,000		$2,200		$44,040
10.			−200						−200E
Bal.	$31,840		$2,200		$12,000		$2,200		$43,840

PART 6

(1)

John's Lawnmower Service
Income Statement
For Year Ended December 31, 1987

Sales..		$22,450
Operating expenses:		
Rent expense..	$4,600	
Advertising expense....................................	3,375	
Utilities expense.......................................	3,000	
Supplies expense	450	
Miscellaneous expense.................................	1,125	12,550
Net income...		$ 9,900

(2)

John's Lawnmower Service
Statement of Owner's Equity
For Year Ended December 31, 1987

Capital, Jan. 1, 1987...		$7,500
Income for the year..	$9,900	
Less drawings for year	8,250	
Increase in owner's equity		1,650
Capital, Dec. 31, 1987		$9,150

(3)

John's Lawnmower Service
Balance Sheet
December 31, 1987

Assets		Liabilities	
Cash	$ 6,000	Accounts payable	$ 1,300
Accounts receivable	3,750	Owner's Equity	
Supplies	700	John Miller, capital	9,150
Total assets	$10,450	Total liabilities & owner's equity	$10,450

CHAPTER 2

PART 1

1. D	**4.** F	**7.** H	**10.** G	**13.** M
2. C	**5.** J	**8.** B	**11.** L	
3. I	**6.** A	**9.** E	**12.** K	

PART 2

1. F	**2.** T	**3.** T	**4.** F	**5.** T
6. F	**7.** F	**8.** T	**9.** T	**10.** F

PART 3

1. b	**2.** a	**3.** d	**4.** c	**5.** a
6. b	**7.** b	**8.** d	**9.** c	**10.** b

PART 4

	Account Debited		Account Credited	
Transaction	Type	Effect	Type	Effect
(1)	asset	+	capital	+
(2)	asset	+	liability	+
(3)	asset	+	liability	+
(4)	liability	−	asset	−
(5)	asset	+	revenue	+
(6)	expense	+	liability	+
(7)	drawing	+	asset	−
(8)	asset	+	asset	−

PART 5

(1) Apr. 3	Cash	11	23,000	
	Equipment	18	15,200	
	Van	19	26,000	
	Ann Lewis, Capital	31		64,200
16	Equipment	18	6,000	
	Accounts Payable	22		6,000
29	Accounts Payable	22	2,800	
	Cash	11		2,800

(2) Account   Cash   Account No. 11

Date	Item	Post. Ref.	Debit	Credit	Balance Debit	Credit
19- Apr. 3		1	23,000		23,000	
29		1		2,800	20,200	

Account   Equipment   Account No. 18

Date	Item	Post. Ref.	Debit	Credit	Balance Debit	Credit
19- Apr. 3		1	15,200		15,200	
16		1	6,000		21,200	

Account   Van   Account No. 19

Date	Item	Post. Ref.	Debit	Credit	Balance Debit	Credit
19- Apr. 3		1	26,000		26,000	

Account   Accounts Payable   Account No. 22

Date	Item	Post. Ref.	Debit	Credit	Balance Debit	Credit
19- Apr. 16		1		6,000		6,000
29		1	2,800			3,200

Account   Ann Lewis, Capital   Account No. 31

Date	Item	Post. Ref.	Debit	Credit	Balance Debit	Credit
19- Apr. 3		1		64,200		64,200

(3)

Ann's Service Co.
Trial Balance
April 30, 19-

	Debit	Credit
Cash	20,200	
Equipment	21,200	
Van	26,000	
Accounts Payable		3,200
Ann Lewis, Capital		64,200
	67,400	67,400

PART 6

(1)

Cash

(1)	50,000	(2)	2,400
(5)	19,600	(3)	1,300
		(4)	2,200
		(6)	6,000
		(7)	1,500
		(8)	3,600
		(9)	800
		(11)	240
		(12)	1,000
		(14)	800
		(15)	6,000

Office Supplies

(3)	1,300	

Prepaid Insurance

(12)	1,000	

Library

(15)	6,000	

Office Equipment				Rent Expense	
(1)	11,600		(2)	2,400	
(13)	3,200				

Auto				Salary Expense	
(6)	24,000		(4)	2,200	

Accounts Payable					Light and Power Expense	
(7)	1,500	(6)	18,000	(10)	240	
(11)	240	(10)	240			
		(13)	3,200			

Tom Teel, Capital				Auto Repairs and Maintenance Expense	
		(1)	61,600	(9)	800

Tom Teel, Drawing				Janitor Expense	
(8)	3,600		(14)	800	

Legal Fees		
	(5)	19,600

(2)

Tom Teel
Trial Balance
January 31, 19-

Cash	43,760	
Office Supplies	1,300	
Prepaid Insurance	1,000	
Library	6,000	
Office Equipment	14,800	
Auto	24,000	
Accounts Payable		19,700
Tom Teel, Capital		61,600
Tom Teel, Drawing	3,600	
Legal Fees		19,600
Rent Expense	2,400	
Salary Expense	2,200	
Light and Power Expense	240	
Auto Repairs and Maintenance Expense	800	
Janitor Expense	800	
	100,900	100,900

CHAPTER 3

PART 1

1. A	5. B	8. J
2. C	6. D	9. G
3. F	7. H	10. I
4. E		

PART 2

1. F	2. F	3. T	4. F	5. T
6. T	7. T	8. F	9. T	10. F

PART 3

1. b	2. c	3. a	4. d	5. c

PART 4

(1)

Cash		
	Apr. 1	5,000

Prepaid Insurance			
Apr. 1	5,000	Dec. 31	1,250

Insurance Expense		
Dec. 31	1,250	

(2) Unexpired insurance $3,750
(3) Insurance expense.. $1,250

PART 5

(1)

Cash		
	Aug. 7	200
	14	200
	21	200
	28	200

Salary Expense		
Aug. 7	200	
14	200	
21	200	
28	200	
31	40	

Salaries Payable		
	Aug. 31	40

(2) Salary expense $840
(3) Salaries payable .... $ 40

PART 6

Journal

19--					
Jan. 31	Sales	47	15,480	
	Income Summary	36		15,480
31	Income Summary	36	12,330	
	Salary Expense	58		7,200
	Supplies Expense	67		5,130

Account	Income Summary					Account No. 36
		Post.			Balance	
Date	Item	Ref.	Debit	Credit	Debit	Credit
19--						
Jan. 31		8		15,480		15,480
31		8	12,330			3,150

Account	Sales					Account No. 47
19--						
Jan. 15		5		4,050		4,050
31		6		11,430		15,480
31		8	15,480			-0-

Account	Salary Expense					Account No. 58
19--						
Jan. 31		6	7,200		7,200	
31		8		7,200	-0-	

Account	Supplies Expense					Account No. 67
19--						
Jan. 15		5	2,340		2,340	
25		6	1,710		4,050	
31		6	1,080		5,130	
31		8		5,130	-0-	

PART 7

(1) and (2)

Rider Service Company
Work Sheet
For Month Ended January 31, 19--

	Trial Balance Dr.	Trial Balance Cr.	Adjustments Dr.	Adjustments Cr.	Adj. Trial Balance Dr.	Adj. Trial Balance Cr.	Income Statement Dr.	Income Statement Cr.	Balance Sheet Dr.	Balance Sheet Cr.
Cash	7,980				7,980				7,980	
Accounts Receivable	6,300				6,300				6,300	
Supplies	2,380			(c) 980	1,400				1,400	
Prepaid Rent	7,560			(b) 630	6,930				6,930	
Tools and Equipment	18,900				18,900				18,900	
Accumulated Depreciation		1,330		(d) 560		1,890				1,890
Accounts Payable		6,160				6,160				6,160
Gayle Rider, Capital		32,410				32,410				32,410
Gayle Rider, Drawing	2,800				2,800				2,800	
Sales		24,850				24,850		24,850		
Salary Expense	13,790		(a) 980		14,770		14,770			
Miscellaneous Expense	5,040				5,040		5,040			
	64,750	64,750								
Salaries Payable				(a) 980		980				980
Rent Expense			(b) 630		630		630			
Supplies Expense			(c) 980		980		980			
Depreciation Expense			(d) 560		560		560			
			3,150	3,150	66,290	66,290	21,980	24,850	44,310	41,440
Net Income							2,870			2,870
							24,850	24,850	44,310	44,310

(3)

Rider Service Company
Income Statement
For Month Ended January 31, 19--

Sales		$24,850
Operating expenses:		
Salary expense	$14,770	
Supplies expense	980	
Rent expense	630	
Depreciation expense	560	
Miscellaneous expense	5,040	
Total operating expenses		21,980
Net income		$ 2,870

Rider Service Company
Statement of Owner's Equity
For Month Ended January 31, 19--

Capital, January 1, 19--		$32,410
Income for the month	$2,870	
Less drawings for the month	2,800	
Increase in owner's equity		70
Capital, January 31, 19--		$32,480

Rider Service Company
Balance Sheet
January 31, 19--

Assets

Current assets:		
Cash	$ 7,980	
Accounts receivable	6,300	
Supplies	1,400	
Prepaid rent	6,930	
Total current assets		$22,610
Plant assets:		
Tools and equipment	$18,900	
Less accumulated		
depreciation	1,890	17,010
Total assets		$39,620

Liabilities

Current liabilities:		
Accounts payable	$ 6,160	
Salaries payable	980	
Total liabilities		$ 7,140

Owner's Equity

Gayle Rider, capital		32,480
Total liabilities and owner's equity		$39,620

CHAPTER 4

PART 1

1. A	**5.** I	**8.** D
2. H	**6.** J	**9.** F
3. C	**7.** E	**10.** G
4. B		

PART 2

1. F	**2.** F	**3.** T	**4.** F	**5.** T
6. F	**7.** T	**8.** T	**9.** T	**10.** F

PART 3

1. b	**2.** d	**3.** b	**4.** a	**5.** c

PART 4

Journal

(1) Purchases	4,000	
Accounts Payable		4,000
(2) Accounts Payable	4,000	
Cash		3,920
Purchases Discounts		80
(3) Purchases	3,000	
Transportation In	80	
Accounts Payable		3,080
(4) Accounts Payable	500	
Purchases Returns and Allowances		500
(5) Accounts Payable	2,580	
Cash		2,530
Purchases Discounts		50

PART 5

Journal

(1) Cash	2,300	
Sales		2,300
(2) Accounts Receivable	3,880	
Sales		3,880
(3) Cash	3,705	
Credit Card Collection Expense	175	
Accounts Receivable		3,880
(4) Accounts Receivable	4,200	
Sales		4,200
Accounts Receivable	125	
Cash		125
(5) Sales Returns and Allowances	300	
Accounts Receivable		300
(6) Cash	3,947	
Sales Discounts	78	
Accounts Receivable		4,025

PART 6

Cost of merchandise sold:			
Merchandise inventory, July 1, 1986			$145,000
Purchases		$480,000	
Less: Purchases returns and allowances	$4,200		
Purchases discounts	5,100	9,300	
Net purchases		$470,700	
Add transportation in		3,300	
Cost of merchandise purchased			474,000
Merchandise available for sale			$619,000
Less merchandise inventory, June 30, 1987			170,000
Cost of merchandise sold			$449,000

PART 7

Gurnee Corporation
Work Sheet
For Year Ended May 31, 19--

	Trial Balance Dr.	Trial Balance Cr.	Adjustments Dr.	Adjustments Cr.	Adj. Trial Balance Dr.	Adj. Trial Balance Cr.	Income Statement Dr.	Income Statement Cr.	Balance Sheet Dr.	Balance Sheet Cr.
Cash	72,900				72,900				72,900	
Accounts Receivable	116,000				116,000				116,000	
Merchandise Inventory	156,390		112,800 (b)	156,390 (a)	112,800				112,800	
Office Supplies	10,250			9,270 (c)	980				980	
Prepaid Insurance	25,740			12,900 (d)	12,840				12,840	
Delivery Equipment	60,200				60,200				60,200	
Accum. Depr.-Del. Equip.		12,900		8,600 (e)		21,500				21,500
Accounts Payable		77,600				77,600				77,600
Capital Stock		135,000				135,000				135,000
Retained Earnings		60,900				60,900				60,900
Income Summary			156,390 (a)	112,800 (b)	156,390	112,800	156,390	112,800		
Sales		1,035,700				1,035,700		1,035,700		
Sales Returns & Allow.	11,000				11,000		11,000			
Purchases	671,900				671,900		671,900			
Purchases Discounts		8,300				8,300		8,300		
Sales Salaries Expense	78,200				78,200		78,200			
Advertising Expense	12,090				12,090		12,090			
Delivery Expense	42,000				42,000		42,000			
Depr. Exp.-Del. Equip.			8,600 (e)		8,600		8,600			
Misc. Selling Expense	13,900				13,900		13,900			
Office Salaries Expense	53,400				53,400		53,400			
Office Supplies Expense			9,270 (c)		9,270		9,270			
Insurance Expense			12,900 (d)		12,900		12,900			
Misc. General Expense	6,430				6,430		6,430			
	1,330,400	1,330,400	299,960	299,960	1,451,800	1,451,800	1,076,080	1,156,800	375,720	295,000
Net Income							80,720			80,720
							1,156,800	1,156,800	375,720	375,720

181

CHAPTER 5

PART 1

1. F	**5.** B	**8.** A
2. J	**6.** D	**9.** H
3. C	**7.** G	**10.** E
4. I		

PART 2

1. F	**2.** F	**3.** T	**4.** T	**5.** T
6. F	**7.** F	**8.** T	**9.** T	**10.** T

PART 3

1. c	**2.** a	**3.** d	**4.** d	**5.** b

PART 4

	19--				
(1) Dec.	31	Salary Expense	611	260	
		Salaries Payable	213		260
(2)	31	Income Summary	313	48,760	
		Salary Expense	611		48,760
(3) Jan.	1	Salaries Payable	213	260	
		Salary Expense	611		260
(4)	4	Salary Expense	611	1,300	
		Salaries Payable	213		1,300

Account	Salaries Payable				Account No. 213	
		Post.			Balance	
Date	Item	Ref.	Debit	Credit	Debit	Credit
19--						
Dec. 31		23		260		260
19--						
Jan. 1		23	260		—	—
4		23		1,300		1,300

Account	Income Summary				Account No. 313
19-- Dec. 31		23	48,760		48,760

Account	Salary Expense				Account No. 611
19-- Dec. 31	Balance	√			48,500
31		23	260		48,760
31		23		48,760	-0-
19-- Jan. 1		23		260	260
4		23	1,300		1,040

PART 5

(1) Adjusting Entries

	19--			
(a)	May 31	Income Summary	156,390	
		Merchandise Inventory		156,390
(b)	31	Merchandise Inventory	112,800	
		Income Summary		112,800
(c)	31	Office Supplies Expense	9,270	
		Office Supplies		9,270
(d)	31	Insurance Expense	12,900	
		Prepaid Insurance		12,900
(e)	31	Depreciation Expense-Delivery Equipment	8,600	
		Accumulated Depreciation-Delivery Equipment		8,600

(2) Closing Entries

19--			
May 31	Sales	1,035,700	
	Purchases Discounts	8,300	
	Income Summary		1,044,000
31	Income Summary	919,690	
	Sales Returns and Allowances		11,000
	Purchases		671,900
	Sales Salaries Expense		78,200
	Advertising Expense		12,090
	Delivery Expense		42,000
	Depreciation Expense-Delivery Equipment		8,600
	Miscellaneous Selling Expense		13,900
	Office Salaries Expense		53,400
	Office Supplies Expense		9,270
	Insurance Expense		12,900
	Miscellaneous General Expense		6,430
31	Income Summary	80,720	
	Retained Earnings		80,720

PART 6

Gurnee Corporation
Income Statement
For Year Ended May 31, 19--

Revenue from sales:		
Sales..	$1,035,700	
Less: Sales returns and allowances	11,000	
Net sales		$1,024,700
Cost of merchandise sold:		
Merchandise inventory, June 1, 19--	$ 156,390	
Purchases $671,900		
Less: Purchases discounts 8,300		
Net purchases.......................................	663,600	
Merchandise available for sale	$ 819,990	
Less: Merchandise inventory, May 31, 19--	112,800	
Cost of merchandise sold...............................		707,190
Gross profit		$ 317,510
Operating expenses:		
Selling expenses:		
Sales salaries expense .... $ 78,200		
Advertising expense.................................... 12,090		
Delivery expense 42,000		
Depreciation expense-delivery		
equipment 8,600		
Miscellaneous selling expense 13,900		
Total selling expenses	$ 154,790	
General expenses:		
Office salaries expense .... $ 53,400		
Office supplies expense.................................. 9,270		
Insurance expense 12,900		
Miscellaneous general expense............................. 6,430		
Total general expenses	82,000	
Total operating expenses		236,790
Net income		$ 80,720

PART 7

(1)

Gurnee Corporation
Balance Sheet
May 31, 19--

Assets

Cash..		$ 72,900
Accounts receivable..		116,000
Merchandise inventory...		112,800
Office supplies..		980
Prepaid insurance...		12,840
Delivery equipment..	$ 60,200	
Less: Accumulated depreciation.......................................	21,500	38,700
Total assets...		$354,220

Liabilities

Accounts payable..		$ 77,600

Stockholders' Equity

Capital stock...	$135,000	
Retained earnings...	141,620	
Total stockholders' equity..		276,620
Total liabilities and stockholders' equity..............................		$354,220

(2)

Gurnee Corporation
Post-Closing Trial Balance
May 31, 19--

Cash..	72,900	
Accounts Receivable...	116,000	
Merchandise Inventory...	112,800	
Office Supplies..	980	
Prepaid Insurance...	12,840	
Delivery Equipment..	60,200	
Accumulated Depreciation-Delivery Equipment..........................		21,500
Accounts Payable..		77,600
Capital Stock...		135,000
Retained Earnings...		141,620
	375,720	375,720

CHAPTER 6

PART 1

1. E	**5.** C	**8.** I
2. G	**6.** B	**9.** F
3. J	**7.** D	**10.** H
4. A		

PART 2

1. T	**2.** T	**3.** F	**4.** T	**5.** F
6. F	**7.** T	**8.** F	**9.** T	**10.** F

PART 3

1. a	**2.** b	**3.** d	**4.** c	**5.** b
6. d	**7.** a	**8.** d	**9.** c	**10.** a

PART 4

(1) Dec. 31 Insurance Expense 3,850

                Prepaid Insurance 3,850

(2)   31 Income Summary 3,850

                Insurance Expense 3,850

Prepaid Insurance				Insurance Expense			
Dec. 31	5,100	Dec. 31	3,850	Dec. 31	3,850	Dec. 31	3,850
	1,250						

Income Summary	
Dec. 31	3,850

186

PART 5

(1) Dec. 31   Prepaid Rent   2,400
                  Rent Expense   2,400

(2)   31   Income Summary.   3,800
                  Rent Expense   3,800

(3) Jan. 1   Rent Expense   2,400
                  Prepaid Rent   2,400

Prepaid Rent			
Dec. 31	2,400	Jan. 1	2,400

Rent Expense			
Dec. 31	6,200	Dec. 31	2,400
		31	3,800
Jan. 1	2,400		6,200

Income Summary	
Dec. 31	3,800

PART 6

(1) Dec. 31   Unearned Rent   3,000
                  Rent Income   3,000

(2)   31   Rent Income   3,000
                  Income Summary.   3,000

Unearned Rent			
Dec. 31	3,000	Oct. 1	36,000
			33,000

Rent Income			
Dec. 31	3,000	Dec. 31	3,000

Income Summary			
		Dec. 31	3,000

PART 7

(1) Dec. 31	Rent Income		70,000	
	Unearned Rent			70,000
(2) 31	Rent Income		14,000	
	Income Summary			14,000
(3) Jan. 1	Unearned Rent		70,000	
	Rent Income			70,000

Unearned Rent				Rent Income				
Jan. 1	70,000	Dec. 31	70,000	Dec. 31	70,000	May 1	84,000	
				31	14,000			
					84,000			
						Jan. 1	70,000	

Income Summary			
		Dec. 31	14,000

PART 8

(1) Dec. 31	Salary Expense		1,250	
	Salaries Payable			1,250
(2) 31	Income Summary		85,250	
	Salary Expense			85,250
(3) Jan. 1	Salaries Payable		1,250	
	Salary Expense			1,250

Salaries Payable				Salary Expense				
Jan. 1	1,250	Dec. 31	1,250	Dec. 31	84,000	Dec. 31	85,250	
				31	1,250			
					85,250			
						Jan. 1	1,250	

Income Summary		
Dec. 31	85,250	

PART 9

(1) Dec.	31	Delivery Service Receivable		900	
		Delivery Service Income			900
(2)	31	Delivery Service Income		4,100	
		Income Summary...			4,100
(3) Jan.	1	Delivery Service Income		900	
		Delivery Service Receivable			900

Delivery Service Receivable			
Dec. 31	900	Jan. 1	900

Delivery Service Income			
Dec. 31	4,100	Dec. 31	3,200
		31	900
			4,100
Jan. 1	900		

Income Summary	
	Dec. 31 4,100

PART 1

1. H	**5.** E	**8.** B
2. G	**6.** D	**9.** I
3. F	**7.** A	**10.** C
4. J		

PART 2

1. F	**2.** T	**3.** F	**4.** F	**5.** T
6. F	**7.** T	**8.** F	**9.** T	**10.** T

PART 3

1. d	**2.** b	**3.** a	**4.** c	**5.** a

PART 4

(1)   Purchases Journal

Date	Account Credited	Post. Ref.	Purchases Dr. Accts. Pay. Cr.
19-			
Nov. 4	Peterson Co.	✔	5,300
13	Quick Corp.	✔	1,150
22	Gudorf Co.	✔	1,850
26	Norris Inc.	✔	4,300
30			12,600
			(511)(211)

(2) and (3)   General Ledger

Accounts Payable		211		Purchases		511
	Nov. 30	12,600		Nov. 30	12,600	

Accounts Payable Ledger

Gudorf Co.				Peterson Co.		
	Nov. 22	1,850			Nov. 4	5,300

Norris Inc.				Quick Corp.		
	Nov. 26	4,300			Nov. 13	1,150

(4) Gudorf Co.	$ 1,850
Norris Inc.	4,300
Peterson Co.	5,300
Quick Corp.	1,150
Total accounts payable	$12,600

PART 5

Purchases Journal

Date	Account Credited	Post. Ref.	Accounts Payable Cr.	Purchases Dr.	Store Supplies Dr.	Office Supplies Dr.
19-						
Mar. 2	Sullivan Co.		12,150	12,150		
8	Cogan Co.		2,200	2,200		
28	Parsons & Co.		625		410	215

Cash Payments Journal

Date	Ck. No.	Account Debited	Post. Ref.	Sundry Accounts Dr.	Accounts Payable Dr.	Purchases Discounts Cr.	Cash Cr.
Mar. 16	30	Cogan Co.			2,200	44	2,156
20	31	Purchases		1,475			1,475
27	32	Sullivan Co.			11,500		11,500

Journal

Date		Post. Ref.	Dr.	Cr.
19-				
Mar. 9	Accounts Payable—Sullivan Co.		650	
	Purchases			650

PART 6

(1) Purchases	5,250	Accounts Payable	7,290
Store Supplies	330		
Office Supplies	560		
Sundry Accounts	1,150		
Debit Totals	7,290	Credit Totals	7,290

(2) Purchases Journal

Date	Post. Ref.	Accounts Payable Cr.	Purchases Dr.	Store Supplies Dr.	Office Supplies Dr.	Sundry Accts. Dr.		
						Acct.	P.R.	Amt.
June 30	✔	520				Store Equip.	121	520
30	✔	7,290	5,250	330	560			1,150
		(211)	(511)	(114)	(115)			

General Ledger

Store Supplies	114
June 30	330

Office Supplies	115
June 30	560

Store Equipment	121
June 30	520

Accounts Payable	211
	June 30	7,290

Purchases	511
June 30	5,250

PART 7

(1)

Sales Journal

Date	Invoice No.	Account Debited	Post. Ref.	Accts. Rec. Dr. Sales Cr.
19-				
Dec. 7	310	Robert Lucas	✓	185
11	325	Jeff Lyle	✓	260
23	360	Pamela Kelly...	✓	470
30	390	David Stark..	✓	125
				1,040
				(113)(411)

(2) and (3)

General Ledger

Accounts Receivable	113
Dec. 31	1,040

Sales	411
	Dec. 31	1,040

Accounts Receivable Ledger

Pamela Kelley	
Dec. 23	470

Robert Lucas	
Dec. 7	185

Jeff Lyle	
Dec. 11	260

David Stark	
Dec. 30	125

(4)

Pamela Kelley	$ 470
Robert Lucas...	185
Jeff Lyle	260
David Stark	125
Total accounts receivable	$1,040

PART 8

Sales Journal   Page 28

Date	Invoice No.	Account Debited	Post. Ref.	Accts. Rec. Dr. Sales Cr.
19-				
Feb. 4	883	Mears Corp.		9,550
5	884	Vogler Inc.		4,700

Cash Receipts Journal   Page 20

Date	Account Credited	Post. Ref.	Sundry Accounts Cr.	Sales Cr.	Accounts Receivable Cr.	Sales Discounts Dr.	Cash Dr.
19-							
Feb. 14	Mears Corp.				8,750	175	8,575
15	Vogler Inc.				4,700	94	4,606
23	Office Supplies		245				245
28	Sales			37,650			37,650

Journal

19-			
Feb. 9	Sales Returns and Allowances...	800	
	Accounts Receivable—Mears Corp..		800

CHAPTER 8

PART 1

1. D	**5.** I	**8.** B
2. C	**6.** H	**9.** F
3. G	**7.** J	**10.** E
4. A		

PART 2

1. F	**2.** T	**3.** F	**4.** T	**5.** T
6. F	**7.** F	**8.** T	**9.** T	**10.** F

PART 3

1. b	**2.** a	**3.** c	**4.** d	**5.** c

PART 4

(1)

Bradshaw Co.
Bank Reconciliation
June 30, 19--

Balance according to bank statement		$ 9,510
Add deposit not recorded		1,850
		$11,360
Deduct outstanding checks:		
No. 255	$ 290	
No. 280	135	
No. 295	710	1,135
Adjusted balance		$10,225
Balance according to depositor's records		$ 8,960
Add: Error in recording Check No. 289	$ 180	
Error in a deposit	540	
Note and interest collected by bank	570	1,290
		$10,250
Deduct bank service charge		25
Adjusted balance		$10,225

(2) June 30 Cash in Bank		1,265	
Miscellaneous General Expense		25	
Vouchers Payable..			180
Accounts Receivable			540
Notes Receivable			500
Interest Income...			70

PART 5

(1)

Voucher Register

Date	Vou. No.	Payee	Date Paid	Ck. No.	Accounts Payable Cr.	Purchases Dr.
6/1	225	Nixon Co.	6/5	710	950	950
6/1	226	Strange Inc.	6/15	712	800	800
6/1	227	Ranger Corp.	6/8	711	1,300	1,300

(2)

Check Register

Date	Ck. No.	Payee	Vou. No.	Accounts Payable Dr.	Purchases Discounts Cr.	Cash in Bank Cr.
6/5	710	Nixon Co.	225	950	19	931
6/8	711	Ranger Corp.	227	1,300	13	1,287
6/15	712	Strange Inc.	226	800		800

PART 6

June 5	Purchases..	3,626	
	Accounts Payable		3,626
9	Purchases..	13,365	
	Accounts Payable..		13,365
19	Accounts Payable..	13,365	
	Cash in Bank		13,365
July 7	Accounts Payable..	3,626	
	Discounts Lost	74	
	Cash in Bank		3,700

PART 7

(1)	Petty Cash	400.00	
	Accounts Payable		400.00
(2)	Accounts Payable	400.00	
	Cash in Bank		400.00
(3)	Office Supplies	72.12	
	Miscellaneous Selling Expense	115.38	
	Miscellaneous General Expense	52.84	
	Cash Short and Over		2.49
	Accounts Payable		237.85
(4)	Accounts Payable	237.85	
	Cash in Bank		237.85

CHAPTER 9

PART 1

1. I	**5.** F	**8.** G
2. E	**6.** B	**9.** A
3. H	**7.** D	**10.** J
4. C		

PART 2

1. F	**2.** T	**3.** T	**4.** F	**5.** F
6. T	**7.** T	**8.** F	**9.** T	**10.** T

PART 3

1. c	**2.** d	**3.** b	**4.** a	**5.** b

PART 4

1. $80.00	**2.** $30.00	**3.** $70.00	**4.** $80.00	**5.** $30.00
6. $200.00	**7.** $200.00			

PART 5

(1)
Face value	$6,000.00
Interest on face value	150.00
Maturity value	6,150.00
Discount on maturity value	131.54
Proceeds	6,018.46

(2)
Face value	$7,000.00
Interest on face value	280.00
Maturity value	7,280.00
Discount on maturity value	297.27
Proceeds	6,982.73

PART 6

(1) Notes Receivable 4,500.00
    Accounts Receivable—Bevo Davis 4,500.00

(2) Cash 4,546.87
    Interest Income 46.87
    Notes Receivable 4,500.00

(3) Accounts Receivable—Bevo Davis 4,646.25
    Cash 4,646.25

(4) Cash 4,677.23
    Interest Income 30.98
    Accounts Receivable—Bevo Davis 4,646.25

(5) Notes Receivable 2,000.00
    Accounts Receivable—Mark Walker 2,000.00

(6) Accounts Receivable—Mark Walker 2,050.00
    Interest Income 50.00
    Notes Receivable 2,000.00

PART 7

(1) Uncollectible Accounts Expense 10,400
    Allowance for Doubtful Accounts 10,400

(2) Uncollectible Accounts Expense 2,600
    Allowance for Doubtful Accounts 2,600

(3) Allowance for Doubtful Accounts 3,300
    Accounts Receivable—Richmond Co. 3,300

(4) Accounts Receivable—Smith Co. 1,900
    Allowance for Doubtful Accounts 1,900

    Cash 1,900
    Accounts Receivable—Smith Co. 1,900

PART 8

(1) Aug. 31   Uncollectible Accounts Expense 325
    Accounts Receivable—R. Lewis 325

(2) Oct. 10   Accounts Receivable—R. Lewis 325
    Uncollectible Accounts Expense 325

    10   Cash 325
    Accounts Receivable—R. Lewis 325

PART 9

$65,000

PART 1

1. F	**5.** D	**8.** G
2. H	**6.** A	**9.** J
3. I	**7.** E	**10.** C
4. B		

PART 2

1. F	**2.** F	**3.** T	**4.** T	**5.** T
6. T	**7.** T	**8.** F	**9.** F	**10.** T

PART 3

1. b	**2.** a	**3.** b	**4.** d	**5.** c

PART 4

(1) Average unit cost: $\dfrac{\$19,320}{200} = \$96.60$

60 units in the inventory @ $96.60 = $5,796.00

(2)

Date Purchased	Units	Price	Total Cost
August 5	5	$110	$ 550
December 21	55	125	6,875
Total	60		$7,425

(3)

	Units	Price	Total Cost
January 20	45	$ 71	$3,195
April 10	15	85	1,275
Total	60		$4,470

(4)

	Units	Price	Total Cost
January 20	5	$ 71	$ 355
April 10	15	85	1,275
December 21	40	125	5,000
Total	60		$6,630

PART 5

	(1) Fifo	(2) Lifo	(3) Average Cost
Sales..	$1,840,000	$1,840,000	$1,840,000
Ending inventory..	359,500	220,000	288,400
Cost of merchandise sold.................................	1,255,600	1,395,100	1,326,700
Gross profit...	584,400	444,900	513,300

Computation of Ending Inventory

	Date Purchased	Units	Price	Total Cost
FIFO:	November 1 ...	3,100	$70	$217,000
	December 1....	1,900	75	142,500
	Total	5,000		$359,500
LIFO:	January 1	5,000	44	$220,000

Average Cost:
  Average Unit Cost: $\dfrac{\$1,615,100}{28,000} = \$57.68$

  $\$57.68 \times 5,000 = \underline{\$288,400}$

PART 6

	Total	
	Cost	Lower of Cost or Market
Commodity A..	$ 3,000	$ 2,700
Commodity B..	3,625	3,625
Commodity C..	2,655	2,475
Commodity D..	1,000	900
Total..	$10,280	$ 9,700

PART 7

(1)

	Cost	Retail
Merchandise inventory, Jan. 1	$123,600	$172,000
Purchases in January (net)...	264,000	474,000
Merchandise available for sale	$387,600	$646,000

Ratio of cost to retail:
  $\dfrac{\$387,600}{\$646,000} = 60\%$

Sales in January (net)		484,000
Merchandise inventory, Jan. 31, at retail		$162,000
Merchandise inventory, Jan. 31, at estimated cost ($162,000 × 60%)		$ 97,200

(2)

Merchandise inventory, January 1		$123,600
Purchases in January (net)		264,000
Merchandise available for sale		$387,600
Sales in January (net)	$484,000	
Less estimated gross profit ($484,000 × 36%)	174,240	
Estimated cost of merchandise sold		309,760
Estimated merchandise inventory, January 31		$ 77,840

CHAPTER 11

PART 1

1. G	**5.** D	**8.** C
2. H	**6.** I	**9.** F
3. J	**7.** B	**10.** A
4. E		

PART 2

1. F	**2.** T	**3.** F	**4.** F	**5.** T
6. T	**7.** F	**8.** T	**9.** F	**10.** T

PART 3

1. c	**2.** a	**3.** a	**4.** c	**5.** d
6. b	**7.** c	**8.** b	**9.** d	**10.** a

PART 4

June 30	Accumulated Depreciation—Truck	12,000	
	Truck	21,400	
	Truck		15,000
	Cash		18,400

PART 5

(1)	June 30	Accumulated Depr.-Truck	12,000	
		Truck	21,500	
		Loss on Disposal of Plant Assets	2,200	
		Truck		15,000
		Cash		20,700
(2)	June 30	Accumulated Depr.-Truck	12,000	
		Truck	23,700	
		Truck		15,000
		Cash		20,700

PART 6

(1) Dec. 31	Depr. Expense–Automobile		3,000	
	Accum. Depr.–Automobile			3,000
Dec. 31	Depr. Expense–Automobile		3,000	
	Accum. Depr.–Automobile			3,000
(2) Dec. 31	Depr. Expense–Automobile		6,000	
	Accum. Depr.–Automobile			6,000
Dec. 31	Depr. Expense–Automobile		750	
	Accum. Depr.–Automobile			750
(3) Dec. 31	Depr. Expense–Automobile		4,800	
	Accum. Depr.–Automobile			4,800
Dec. 31	Depr. Expense–Automobile		1,200	
	Accum. Depr.–Automobile			1,200

PART 7

Dec. 31	Depreciation Expense–Equipment	3,600	
	Accum. Depreciation–Equipment		3,600

PART 8

Dec. 31	Depreciation Expense–Equipment	14,280	
	Accum. Depreciation–Equipment		14,280

PART 9

Dec. 31	Accum. Depreciation–Fixtures	5,450	
	Cash	1,800	
	Fixtures		6,700
	Gain on Disposal of Assets		550

PART 10

Dec. 31	Depletion Expense	96,500	
	Accum. Depletion–Mineral Rights		96,500

PART 11

Dec. 31	Amortization of Patents	18,500	
	Patents		18,500

CHAPTER 12

PART 1

1. I	**5.** G	**8.** D
2. J	**6.** B	**9.** A
3. E	**7.** F	**10.** H
4. C		

PART 2

1. F	**2.** T	**3.** F	**4.** T	**5.** T
6. T	**7.** F	**8.** T	**9.** T	**10.** F

PART 3

1. b	**2.** c	**3.** d	**4.** a	**5.** d

PART 4

1. $ 75	**2.** $720	**3.** $624

PART 5

(1) Jan. 14	Sales Salaries Expense	29,000	
	Office Salaries Expense	11,000	
	FICA Tax Payable		3,000
	Employees Income Tax Payable		3,200
	Union Dues Payable		900
	United Way Payable		800
	Salaries Payable		32,100
(2) Jan. 14	Salaries Payable	32,100	
	Cash		32,100
(3) Jan. 14	Payroll Taxes Expense	4,400	
	FICA Tax Payable		3,000
	State Unemployment Tax Payable		1,080
	Federal Unemployment Tax Payable		320

PART 6

(1)   B = .08 ($600,000)
          B = $48,000

(2)   B = .08($600,000−B)
          B = $48,000−.08B
    1.08B = $48,000
          B = $44,444.44

(3)   B = .08($600,000−T)
          T = .40($600,000−B)
          B = .08[$600,000−.40($600,000−B)]
          B = .08($600,000−$240,000+.40B)
          B = $48,000−$19,200+.032B
    .968B = $28,800
          B = $29,752.07

(4)   B = .08($600,000−B−T)
          T = .40($600,000−B)
          B = .08[$600,000−B−.40($600,000−B)]
          B = .08($600,000−B−$240,000+.40B)
          B = $48,000−.08B−$19,200+.032B
    1.048B = $28,800
          B = $27,480.92

PART 7

Employee	Annual Earnings	Employee's FICA Tax	Employer's Taxes FICA	State Unemployment	Federal Unemployment	Total
Conkle	$ 48,000	$3,375	$3,375	$189	$ 56	$3,620
Jacka	6,000	450	450	162	48	660
Kogen	8,000	600	600	189	56	845
Schmid	40,000	3,000	3,000	189	56	3,245
	$102,000	$7,425	$7,425	$729	$216	$8,370

PART 8

(1) Dec. 31 Vacation Pay Expense 6,300
              Vacation Pay Payable 6,300

(2) Dec. 31 Product Warranty Expense 2,800
              Product Warranty Payable 2,800

(3) Dec. 31 Pension Expense 41,000
              Cash 27,000
              Unfunded Accrued Pension Cost 14,000

PART 9

(1) Cash 8,000

    Notes Payable 8,000

(2) Notes Payable 8,000

    Interest Expense 240

        Cash 8,240

(3) Cash 6,790

    Interest Expense 210

        Notes Payable 7,000

(4) Notes Payable 7,000

        Cash 7,000

CHAPTER 13

PART 1

1. A	**5.** J	**8.** C	
2. F	**6.** G	**9.** H	
3. D	**7.** I	**10.** B	
4. E			

PART 2

1. F	**8.** F	**15.** T	**22.** F
2. F	**9.** F	**16.** F	**23.** F
3. T	**10.** T	**17.** T	**24.** T
4. F	**11.** F	**18.** T	**25.** T
5. T	**12.** T	**19.** T	**26.** T
6. T	**13.** T	**20.** F	**27.** F
7. T	**14.** F	**21.** T	**28.** F

PART 3

1. b	**2.** c	**3.** a	**4.** d	**5.** c
6. a	**7.** d	**8.** b	**9.** d	**10.** a

PART 4

(1) $100,000

(2) $2,800

(3) $294,000

(4) $567,000

(5) $7,000

PART 5

(1) $2,040,000

(2) $1,430,000

(3) $610,000

PART 6

$60,900

(1) $(2,900)

(2) $(3,400)

(3) $54,600

PART 7

$33,000
(1) (a)   23
(b)   (12)
(c)   (16)
(d)   (5)
(e) $32,990

(2) Materiality

CHAPTER 14

PART 1

1. C   5. E   8. G
2. F   6. D   9. I
3. H   7. J   10. B
4. A

PART 2

1. T	2. T	3. T	4. F	5. F
6. F	7. T	8. T	9. T	10. F
11. T	12. F	13. F	14. F	15. T
16. T	17. F	18. F	19. T	20. T

PART 3

1. b   2. d   3. d   4. a   5. c

PART 4

Cash	430,000	
Merchandise Inventory	60,000	
R. P. Clemens, Capital		490,000

Cash	135,000	
Land	270,000	
Equipment	60,000	
Merchandise Inventory	45,000	
D. J. Sullivan, Capital		510,000

PART 5

(1) Farris' Share	$ 60,000
Shannon's Share	60,000
Total	$120,000

(2) Farris' Share	$ 48,000
Shannon's Share	72,000
Total	$120,000

(3) Farris' Share			$ 40,000
Shannon's Share			80,000
Total			$120,000

	Farris	Shannon	Total
(4) Salary allowance	$45,000	$25,000	$ 70,000
Remaining income	25,000	25,000	50,000
Net income	$70,000	$50,000	$120,000
(5) Interest allowance	$20,000	$40,000	$ 60,000
Remaining income	30,000	30,000	60,000
Net income	$50,000	$70,000	$120,000
(6) Salary allowance	$12,000	$18,000	$ 30,000
Interest allowance	20,000	40,000	60,000
Remaining income	15,000	15,000	30,000
Net income	$47,000	$73,000	$120,000
(7) Salary allowance	$35,000	$37,000	$ 72,000
Interest allowance	20,000	40,000	60,000
Total	$55,000	$77,000	$132,000
Excess of allowances over income	(6,000)	(6,000)	(12,000)
Net income	$49,000	$71,000	$120,000

PART 6

(1) June 30	Vernon, Capital		25,000	
	Parrott, Capital		15,000	
	Forrest, Capital		5,000	
	Keith, Capital			45,000
(2) July 1	Cash		65,000	
	Goodwill		30,000	
	Baker, Capital			95,000

PART 7

(1) Inventory		12,000	
Abbott, Capital			4,000
Bowling, Capital			4,000
Cruz, Capital			4,000
Cruz, Capital		64,000	
Abbott, Capital			64,000
(2) Inventory		9,000	
Abbott, Capital			3,000
Bowling, Capital			3,000
Cruz, Capital			3,000
Cruz, Capital		63,000	
Cash			63,000

PART 8

	Cash +	Noncash Assets =	Liabilities +	Capital		
				Tinker +	Evers +	Chance
(1) Balances before realization	$100,000	$200,000	$60,000	$80,000	$50,000	$110,000
Sale of noncash assets and division of gain	+270,000	−200,000		+21,000	+35,000	+14,000
Balances after realization	$370,000	-0-	$60,000	$101,000	$85,000	$124,000
Payment of liabilities	−60,000		−60,000			
Balances	$310,000		-0-	$101,000	$85,000	$124,000
Distribution of cash to partners	−310,000			−101,000	−85,000	−124,000
Balances	-0-	-0-	-0-	-0-	-0-	-0-
(2) Balances before realization	$100,000	$200,000	$60,000	$ 80,000	$50,000	$110,000
Sale of noncash assets and division of loss	+40,000	−200,000		−48,000	−80,000	−32,000
Balances after realization	$140,000	-0-	$60,000	$ 32,000	$30,000 Dr.	$78,000
Payment of liabilities	−60,000		−60,000			
Balances	$ 80,000		-0-	$ 32,000	$30,000 Dr.	$78,000
Division of deficiency				−18,000	+30,000	−12,000
Balances	$ 80,000		-0-	$ 14,000	-0-	$ 66,000
Distribution of cash to partners	− 80,000			−14,000		−66,000
Final balances	-0-	-0-	-0-	-0-	-0-	-0-

(3) Cash 40,000
    Loss and Gain on Realization 160,000
        Noncash Assets 200,000

    Tinker, Capital 48,000
    Evers, Capital 80,000
    Chance, Capital... 32,000
        Loss and Gain on Realization 160,000

    Liabilities 60,000
        Cash 60,000

    Tinker, Capital 18,000
    Chance, Capital... 12,000
        Evers, Capital 30,000

    Tinker, Capital 14,000
    Chance, Capital... 66,000
        Cash 80,000